THE WORKING WHIPPET

THE WORKING WHIPPET

HELEN HANSELL

Quiller

Copyright © 2010 Helen Hansell

First published in the UK in 2010
by Quiller, an imprint of Quiller Publishing Ltd

British Library Cataloguing-in-Publication Data
A catalogue record for this book
is available from the British Library

ISBN 978 1 84689 067 3

Printed in China

Quiller

An imprint of Quiller Publishing Ltd
Wykey House, Wykey, Shrewsbury, SY4 1JA
Tel: 01939 261616 Fax: 01939 261606
E-mail: info@quillerbooks.com
Website: www.countrybooksdirect.com

Contents

ACKNOWLEDGEMENT

With thanks to my husband Simon for everything he has taught me and for all we have learnt together. And to my whole family for their patience, support, help and advice.

INTRODUCTION

A fit, healthy whippet is a beautiful thing to look on. With their elegance they grace whatever company they keep. They, or rather dogs of their type, have been used by artists and in works of art for centuries. A whippet is beautiful when stationary, a work of art when in full stride and a true spectacle when in pursuit. But beauty, after all, really is only skin deep and there is so much more to the whippet than looks alone.

They are a working dog, one of the best. This book is about celebrating the breed's ability to course and catch rabbits, and about how to draw out and develop this ability in the individual dog. Coursing here, of course, refers to the whippet's excellence at hunting by sight and not by scent. This is not to be confused with the far narrower and exclusive definition of the term to cover coursing under rules when dogs were matched against each other with points awarded for their speed and ability to turn hares. Although, when legal, they did of course excel at this too. The whippet deserves far greater recognition for his work in the field than they have received. This is, after all, what the modern whippet was developed and bred for. With a better appreciation of the origins of the breed and the function for which it was bred, we will be better equipped to give our whippets the life they deserve and give ourselves the working dog of a lifetime.

Although it was not until 1890 that the whippet was officially recognised by the Kennel Club, dogs of the size, type and function of the modern day whippet have been around for centuries, if not millennia. The writer of the oldest work on hunting in the English language, Edward, Duke of York, in *The Master of Game* (1413), wrote, 'The good greyhound should be of middle size, neither too big nor too little, and then he is good for all beasts. If he is too big he is nought for small beasts, and if he were too little he were nought for the great beasts'. And although they may have appeared in paintings, sculptures and bronzes for centuries, it was not until the late nineteenth century that we have written evidence of the existence of a sporting dog bearing the name 'whippet' and doing what a whippet does best; chase and catch rabbits.

Working with hunting dogs fulfils a deep, almost primeval need to be in touch with the countryside and to be a part of all that goes on there. We humans have long since lost ability to do that ourselves. The best we can hope for is a vicarious enjoyment in being part of a team with our dog. Over the years many breeds have been developed to do different jobs. Whether it is finding, fetching or coursing and catching, all of them in their own special ways enable us to get on terms with our quarry. If the latter method is your chosen sport, you have chosen well. You would be hard pressed to do better than to take on a whippet as your hunting companion. The whippet is perfectly equipped for the task of taking our most common mammal, the rabbit, in truly magnificent fashion

This book is both a celebration of the working whippet and a tool. It describes the methods I have found that work well for me and my dogs. This book is not the definitive guide; it is merely a guide to be read through, picked up, put down, argued against and, I hope, agreed with too. All dogs, like the people who own them, are individuals, and all need slightly different techniques to bring out the best in them. This is a handbook for those who want to do just that in their whippet. It is not to be followed slavishly but to be thought about and to be thought-provoking.

1 THE IDEAL WORKING WHIPPET

To have taken the time and trouble to have picked up this book and perhaps even paid for it out of your own pocket, I am assuming that you are serious in your desire to work your dog. Perhaps you already have a whippet or perhaps you have taken the decision to get one. Whatever your situation and whatever the stage you and your dog are at, I am going to start at the very beginning. We are going right back to those early and exciting days when you set out to find and pick a young puppy.

I am also assuming that catching rabbits is your game for the whippet really is the rabbiting dog par excellence. True, they can put up a good show against other quarry. They can enjoy a bit of ratting and have been known to take to foxes with remarkable gusto, when it was legal for them to do so of course. But everything about the whippet says speed and subtlety. Why squander these on the kinds of quarry that can be far better and more safely tackled by other breeds? If you have spent money on a well-bred working whippet and gone to the effort of training it, you will want to keep it for the serious and, at times, truly spectacular business of pursuing the rabbit.

And why are whippets as a breed so very adept at catching rabbits? Well, quite simply, the good ones have everything it takes to take a rabbit. They have speed, because rabbits are fast; they have agility because rabbits can twist and turn in mid-stride; they possess the brain to anticipate when this is going to happen and to read the ground; and an intelligence that allows them to learn from the mistakes as well as the successes. Add to the mix a tough constitution, because coursing any animal over the ground is a risky business, and you have a winning formula.

It is obvious to all that the whippet is a dog born and bred to run. Its lean, muscular elegance tells the story. But we can break it down just that bit more, and learn quite a bit in the process.

The Whippet Breed Standard

This is surely the best place to start for it lays down exactly how the ideal whippet should look. And in the whippet, form and function are so intimately linked that whether destined for work or for the less strenuous exertions of showing, the closer our whippets conform to this standard, the better. However, repetition without explanation is of little use to either man or beast. Whippets are the rabbit dogs par excellence: and to be worthy of this glorious title, the whippet's body and brain must possess certain qualities and characteristics.

A fit whippet is a beautiful sight.

GENERAL APPEARANCE
Balanced combination of muscular power and strength with elegance and grace of outline. Built for speed and work. All forms of exaggeration should be avoided.

If you have any involvement with horses, and especially the finer, racier breeds, you will have a head start when it comes to assessing the whippet's conformation as the basic principles for speed, strength and movement apply equally to the dog's physique as they do to that of the horse. And while many horse riders are familiar with the 'points of the horse', indeed can point to them, and understand the contribution they make to their horse's overall way of going and suitability for work, few dog owners (greyhound and whippet race trainers, owners and followers excepted) are as conversant with the dog's conformation and physique. With experience comes an eye for a dog (or horse for that matter) and the ability to tell at a glance whether an animal will make good or not. Farmers call it 'stock sense'. And although some seem to have a more natural ability to observe and analyse their animals, to others it is a more hardly won talent. Whether you fall into the former or the latter category, we can all be helped by learning some of the basic features of the dog's physique and how they relate to his performance in the field.

CHARACTERISTICS
An ideal companion. Highly adaptable in domestic and sporting surroundings.

HEAD AND SKULL
Long and lean, flat on top, tapering to muzzle with slight stop, rather wide between the eyes, jaws powerful and clean-cut, nose black. In blues, a bluish colour is permitted, liver noses in creams and other dilute colours, in whites or part-colours a butterfly nose is permissible.

It may well be true that handsome is as handsome does but a whippet should always be pleasing to the eye. Part of the charm of the breed is its beauty and grace and even the most elegant of dogs with the most beautifully sculpted of bodies can be ruined by an unrefined head. There is really no reason why a dog should not be good looking as well as good at working.

EYES
Oval, bright, expression very alert.

EARS
Rose shaped, small, fine in texture.

MOUTH
Jaws strong with a perfect, regular and complete scissor bite, i.e. upper teeth closely overlapping lower teeth and set square to the jaws.

NECK
Long, muscular, elegantly arched.

FOREQUARTERS
Shoulders well laid back with flat muscles. Moderate space between the shoulder blades at the withers. The upper arm is approximately of equal length to the shoulder, placed so that the elbow falls directly under the withers when viewed in profile. Forearms straight and upright with moderate bladed bone. Front not too wide. Pasterns strong with slight spring.

BODY
Chest very deep with plenty of heart room. Well filled in front. Brisket deep. Broad, well-muscled back, firm, somewhat long, showing graceful arch over the loin but not humped. Ribs well sprung. Loin giving impression of strength and power. Definite tuck up.

This well-sprung rib cage is important for more than just cosmetic reasons. A whippet with a well-rounded barrel-like chest has plenty of room for his powerful heart and lungs to work at their maximum capacity. Dogs that lack this large engine room are less likely to thrive and more likely to lack the stamina a working dog needs to excel.

HINDQUARTERS
Strong and broad across thighs, with well-developed second thighs, stifles well bent without exaggeration with hocks well let down. Able to stand naturally over a lot of ground.

Great driving power is needed to power a whippet at speed.

FEET
Oval, well split up between toes, knuckles well arched, pads thick, nails strong.

These parts of a whippet's anatomy are all too often overlooked and yet they are of crucial importance to the dog performance and overall soundness. Feet are admittedly not a very glamorous topic but good feet are absolutely vital to health and ability of the individual dog. The familiar phrase, 'no foot no horse' can be equally said about the running dog. And although you can do a lot to prepare, improve and maintain your dog's feet, inherently bad conformation here will almost invariably lead to trouble later. Lameness, either in the foot itself, or further up in the leg can result and there can be few things more frustrating, both to man and dog, than a lame running dog.

TAIL
No feathering. Long, tapering, reaching at least to the hock. When in action carried in a delicate curve not higher than the back.

Whippets need a good length of tail to help them maintain their balance when turning and twisting in pursuit or in play, and also when they are travelling at great speed over uneven ground.

GAIT/ MOVEMENT
Should possess great freedom of action. In profile should move with a long, easy stride whilst holding the topline. The forelegs should be thrown forward and low over the ground. Hind legs should come well under the body giving greater propelling power. General movement not to look stilted, high stepping, short or mincing. True coming and going.

COLOUR
Any colour or mixture of colours.

SIZE
Desirable height: dogs 47-51 cms (18 ½-20 ins); bitches: 44-47 cms (17 ½-18 ½ ins).

Most whippets, especially those bred primarily for work, actually exceed these height categories. It is far more usual to find bitches standing at around the 19 or 20 inch mark and dogs standing at about 21 to 22 inches at the shoulder. Even in the show ring whippets that exceed the height standard are now being seen and frequently being placed. There has undeniably been a trend towards bigger dogs but bigger isn't always better. True, there are advantages, the taller dog sees more and takes longer strides, and has more bone and substance to take the knocks. But, the very essence of the whippet is the greatest speed and stamina in the smallest frame. The whippet is after all, economy personified.

And finally to faults, for it is as well to know what is undesirable as well as desirable in the breed.

FAULTS
Any departure from the foregoing points should be considered a fault and

the seriousness with which the fault should be regarded should be in exact proportion to its degree and its effect upon the health and welfare of the dog.

Male animals should have two apparently normal testicles fully descended into the scrotum.

Copyright: The Kennel Club
Reproduced with their permission

So we can see that physically at least, most dogs bred to show and dogs from show breeding would be capable of coursing a rabbit. Mentally, however, not many could take the knocks that the working dog deals with every day and come back wanting more. Not many could out-think their quarry, anticipating their next move, and the one after that too. Few would have the drive, the determination and the stamina that the truly exceptional working dog needs. How could they when generation after generation have had to do nothing more taxing than walk prettily on a lead and stand well to be judged?

I have nothing against show dogs, it is just that I would not want one in my kennels. When the terrain gets more challenging, when the weather takes a turn for the worse, when the quarry are at their savviest and streetwise best, then the difference between show whippets and working ones becomes all too apparent. It is then that all those qualities that can't be seen on the show bench – the desire to hunt, the drive to go the distance, and then some, the toughness and determination – come to the fore. As the old saw goes, when the going gets tough, the tough get going.

The dogs this book is devoted to have this extra toughness. They have an innate desire to hunt and the will to do so with a drive, determination and courage that is remarkable. These are the dogs that have been bred to run and to course. These are the working whippets. Their natural instincts have been honed and strengthened down the generations. They have been tried and tested on the coursing field and proved their worth. Now, you're never going to get a whippet that will smash its way through a clump of brambles or a blackthorn thicket, just on the off chance that a rabbit might be tucked away somewhere or a pheasant lying low in the cover. But if there really is quarry for the pot tucked away then a good whippet, bred and prepared for its job, will find it and do its best to put it in the bag for you. A particularly driven whippet bitch I once owned swam a river to course a rabbit on the opposite bank.

So how do you find your pot-filling paragon? You put in thought, patience and care. Just because a bloke in the pub has 'a mate who has a litter of whippet pups in the garden shed' doesn't mean you should buy one of them. And just because this particular garden shed happens to be a few minutes drive away, it doesn't mean this will be the pup that will grow into the whippet you want. Even harder to resist is the 'mate' who brings one of his pups to the pub with him to tempt you with his wares. There are few things as appealing as a young pup or more alluring to the dog man than the idea of bringing on a new dog. But, there is much wisdom in the old saying, 'Buy in haste, repent at leisure.' You may well happen upon a nice little pup. But chances are he has no papers, no pedigree, no background, and you are lucky if you even have his breeder's telephone number to ask about these things. True, a pedigree isn't everything but it is much better than nothing if you want to know where your dog has come from and just what he might be capable of.

Whippets can come to terms with rabbits even on their home turf.

Not only might you lose money (almost certain once cost of travel, worming, vaccination etc. is taken into account) but you will have to begin your search all over again (if you haven't lost heart after the disappointment). Do your homework. Unlike retrievers and spaniels that have the opportunity to prove their worth in field trials, there is no such formal and established standard for assessing the running dog's ability. Those trying to sell you a puppy or get a stud fee are not necessarily the most impartial assessors of their dog's ability or suitability for breeding. Take your time and do a lot of talking. In an ideal world, we would know both parents, have seen them work, by day and at night, watched their behaviour with other dogs, while travelling, in the house, in the kennel. In this wonderful world, there would also be world peace, an end to poverty and everybody would live happily ever after. But in our far from perfect world, we shall just have to do our best and make the best of the opportunities we have.

Now some people seem peculiarly reluctant to take on a puppy and spend their lives buying and, more often than not, selling older dogs when they don't come up to scratch. Now I can understand anybody's reluctance to deal with all the downsides and difficulties of bringing on a young puppy. It's not easy bringing on a young dog or rather it's not easy bringing a young dog on well. Any fool can take a puppy and feed him. Making him an enjoyable companion alone takes time, turning him into a competent and reliable working companion requires even more effort and patience.

House-training is enough to try the patience of some. Whippets are by nature very clean and fastidious dogs and soon learn to keep the house clean. But the discipline involved in instilling these basic rules into one of the most compliant of breeds defeats quite a few. If you are one of those (and I consider that to be highly unlikely if you have taken the time and trouble to pick up this book and read this far) perhaps you are better leaving the puppy with his dam and looking instead for an older dog. Better for the puppy that is, for despite the large number of lurchers and running dogs out there for sale, few will do their new owner proud. As already mentioned producing a good dog involves many hours work, and a fair bit of money. Unless absolutely desperate (and I have known people lose their homes before their dogs) anyone who has invested such a great deal of their waking hours, and made a good job of it, will be loath to let their dog go, let alone for some of the ridiculously low sums you see advertised. Be wary of older dogs, they almost all come with problems. Be it yapping, hunting up, stock-chasing, ferret-hating, they are all things that not only could you do without, but that can be easily prevented if you rear and train your own dog properly. If a job's worth doing, it's worth doing properly. Get a puppy, and get a good one.

And if you have a choice, I recommend getting your puppy in the summer months. Obviously, you might not be fortunate enough to be able to pick your timing. You may even have to book a puppy from a particular mating if you are to be in with a chance of getting your hands on one, especially if it is a bitch that you want (more of that later) But long summer days just make it that bit easier to spend time with your puppy out in the garden, and to get out and about in general. This is particularly important if you keep your dog outdoors and your time together is subsequently limited. True, you can always make the time and you can always take the pup indoors with you of an evening. But, as they say, the road to hell is paved with good intentions, and with the best will in the world it is not always easy to get your dog indoors with you. Some spouses, for example, seem curiously reluctant to allow that 'smelly dog' into their sweet-smelling home. If you have a less fussy partner, count your blessings. If your puppy is indoors from the beginning, it matters less what time of year they join the family. Indeed, it might even be better to acquire such a dog during the winter when bad weather and dark days and evenings limit the distractions available.

Whatever the time of year, you have decided on a whippet and you have decided to take on a puppy. How do you begin this exciting quest? Well, you take your time for a start. Before you pick up the phone and start calling up about all the whippet puppies you see advertised, ask yourself a few questions, and answer them honestly. What do you expect and want from your dog? Be honest and be realistic. Do you want your dog to do a bit of everything? Will they be kept in the house or kennel? Will you be out most by day or at night? You might like the idea of heading off every week-end with a whippet by your side and a ferret in your pocket. If family commitments make nights out lamping a more practical propositions, you might have to make a few compromises. Now although one of the (many) great things about whippets, both dogs and bitches, is their ability to put up a good show, whatever you ask them to do, there are occasions and circumstances where a dog or bitch might just have the edge over the opposite sex.

Take lamping for example. That little bit of extra height that a dog has compared to a bitch can make reaching down to the slip lead just that little bit easier. During the course of one night you might not notice the difference; after a full season you'll appreciate it; after several you'll know what I'm talking about. Plus the longer stride of the larger male makes for better runs on the lamp when the rabbits are two to three hundred yards away. The smaller stature of the whippet bitch might just help her work on and around the warren and might enable her to be just that fraction sharper off the mark on short chases. The difference is marginal but it is still worth taking into consideration before you buy a dog (or a bitch) that could be with you for the next ten or so years.

I much prefer dogs in the house. Now I am far from house proud but when bitches come in season, as they do twice a year, they can be very messy indeed. In fact, I prefer dogs all round but I'm in the minority as the price of puppies proves. Bitches, of any breed, are nearly always more expensive than dogs. There is a widespread belief that bitches are easier to handle and train than dogs. In some breeds this is certainly the case but in whippets there really is very little difference between the sexes are far as temperament goes. Dogs are just as biddable and perhaps even a little more level-headed than bitches. I know that the most driven and unusually bull-headed whippet I ever had was a black bitch. For the first eighteen months of her life she was virtually unstoppable but for the next ten years was the best working dog I have ever had the privilege of owning, of any breed.

Perhaps whippet bitches are more popular because buyers hope and assume they'll make a bit of money down the line breeding a litter. Perhaps they will, but it is unlikely if they set out to do the job properly. First there is the stud fee, the cost of travelling to and from said dog (fuel doesn't come cheap these days and few of us are lucky enough to have the perfect working whippet standing at stud just down the road – if only we were!) Assuming the bitch catches, she has to be well fed, wormed and cared for up to, during and after she whelps. Puppies need a heat lamp for the first few weeks, even if they are born indoors. That means at least two infra-red lamps and bulbs (one in use and one kept as a spare) and a hike in your electricity bill.

Then there is food and worming for the puppies, vaccinations, registrations with the Kennel Club, advertising etc. The list goes on and on. Don't get me wrong, I have nothing against people breeding from their dogs, and even profiting from it, just so long as they think carefully about what it involves in terms of time, effort and expense before they embark upon it. Be clear about what you want your whippet for and think carefully about whether you really do have the time and inclination to breed a litter that will do credit to the breed as well as yourself. Buying a bitch solely on the 'off-chance' that you might one day have a litter from her is not a good enough reason.

Something few people seem to consider when breeding a litter is the time and effort needed to get a bitch back into shape for working. It takes time and there is never a good time for a good working dog to be out of action. Carrying puppies, whelping a litter, producing enough milk so that they thrive, is a tiring and physically taxing event for a bitch. It takes time to recover and regain fitness, mentally as well as physically and that means if you only have the one dog, time out from working for both of you.

But back to the subject in hand, picking your puppy. In short, the whippet's overall appearance should be pleasing to the eye. In all, he should convey an image of lean, slender, muscular strength. Ideally, you would also be able to view a full sibling to the puppy you're thinking about buying because that gives you the best guide as to what this pairing of whippets is capable of producing.

First impressions do count. If you're going to spend a lot of time together, it helps if you at least start out with a liking for each other And as it can be hard to see what you are getting in an eight-week-old puppy, you will need to spend a bit of time examining and assessing the parents. When setting out to pick a puppy, it is far easier to examine the conformation of the parents than to assess an eight-week-old puppy which, after all, still has a huge amount of developing left to do. This is why it is so important to see the parents, ideally both the dam and the sire.

Don't just settle for seeing them behind a kennel door or passing through the kitchen either. You will need to take stock of her character as well as her physique. The dam will not look in the peak of fitness. Producing and rearing a litter of pups is physically and mentally draining and if she has done her job well then she is more than entitled to look a little weary. However be wary of a bitch that looks decidedly under the weather and/or sorry for herself. Such an appearance suggests many things, none of them good. She may be ill, she may not have received enough of the right food or she might have an overly nervous disposition. All of these could have an impact on the puppy you are considering taking home. Whatever the cause, you should think carefully about buying a puppy from such a background. Assuming the bitch has nothing wrong with her that a few weeks of recovery time won't put right, what are the qualities a dam should possess?

What you are looking for in any working dog is a good, sound conformation and a friendly outgoing attitude to life. She should appear generally in proportion, and she should move well. You don't have to watch her behind a rabbit at full stretch to assess her movement either. The walk is usually a fairly good indicator of how well the dog moves at a faster pace. Strides should be even, long and straight and convey an image of free and easy movement.

You are looking for a kind eye, a look that promises loyalty and a willingness to give their all to please you, to keep going when others falter. That is what you are paying for when you buy a well-bred working whippet.

Whippets are fast dogs, but some are faster than others. Why that should be so depends not only on fitness, feeding and preparation but also on a dog's basic conformation. Speed=length of stride x frequency of stride. It's a simple equation and one that can be worked out by looking at an individual dog. For a good long stride we need a good long sloping shoulder to allow the forearm/leg to extend as far as possible. The hindquarters too have their part to play in powering the stride forward. Here we want a good length of leg for leverage. Front and rear ends of this running machine must be joined by a good long back. This will dictate more than anything how much ground a dog can cover at full stretch. Long backs are more important than long legs for a long stride. And remember that although a big dog looks slower he will actually move faster as his longer strides literally eat up the ground.

Of course, there are always certain individuals with unpromising conformations that seem to defy all expectations and show a remarkable turn of speed, strength and stamina, but these are rare creatures indeed and are the

A whippet in full stride.

exceptions that really do prove the rule. A dog with serious faults will always be more prone to physical problems – strains, sprains and lameness. But, remember no dog is perfect and many minor conformation faults can safely be overlooked without later going on to cause major problems.

Something many people neglect to examine but is of fundamental importance to the working ability of the whippet is the feet. We all want to know whether the dew claws have been removed as they most certainly should be, but I'm always surprised when I breed a litter how few prospective purchasers look any further down the leg. But the conformation and the condition of the feet themselves are of great importance. To paraphrase a famous old saying: 'No foot, no dog'. A tremendous amount of stress and strain is put on the running dog's legs and feet. The only thing you can do to minimise this is to start off with a dog that has a good, sound conformation. A lame dog catches little and is a source of permanent frustration to owner and dog alike. There are likely to be enough occasions over the life of a working whippet where injuries might result in enforced rest without beginning with a weakness. Splayed toes are ugly as well as ineffective. Tight bunched toes are inefficient shock absorbers. What you are looking for is a compact and neatly formed foot capable of carrying the dog at great speeds over uneven ground and taking the knocks that a lifetime of work inevitably entails.

A word of warning. In recent years the demand for and consequently the price of whippets has risen considerably. There are always cowboys around but they seem to multiply when they think there's some money to be made. While I wouldn't suggest anyone was put off by a workaday set up, I would strongly recommend that you refuse to buy any puppy from any litter that has not been bred and reared properly. Don't let pity or embarrassment force you to buy from anyone who has not done their job. They don't deserve a penny of you hard-earned cash. And you won't be helping the dogs either. The more puppies that are sold the more likely they are to breed again, inflicting more misery on the dam and her puppies, and producing animals that are of no credit to the breed or breeder. Incidentally, I never sell a puppy to anyone who haggles over the price. If someone isn't prepared to pay for a puppy, they are unlikely to care for it either. 'Easy come, easy go' sadly applies to dogs. So don't insult a good breeder by asking for fifty quid off. Just count yourself lucky you have the chance to get hold of a good dog that will give you its best all its life.

So you've established that the breeding is all that you could wish for (and remember there are no guarantees or certainties in animal breeding; it is what makes it perennially exciting and occasionally frustrating). Of course, you will always find someone who has bred brilliant dogs from unpromising parents. Good on them and good for them. If you want to rely on luck to produce a good dog, then by all means go for this approach. If instead you want a bit more certainty, then look at and understand your dog's pedigree. An ancestry of proven dogs is the best guarantee you can get when it comes to breeding, buying and working animals.

Now to the puppy itself. Much of your work in picking a puppy will be done before you even see the litter. If you have children, and a hard heart, leave them at home if you want to have a free hand in choosing your puppy. Small children have a particular penchant for the smallest, shyest puppy in the litter. True, the runt sometimes turns into a tough and feisty little character, but often they don't amount to anything much at all. Size and boldness at eight weeks old is no guarantee of future prowess but it is a better indication than anything else at this stage of development.

So what about colour? To some people it is of fundamental importance. Others care little. A good dog, they argue, is never a bad colour. One thing is for sure, colour is not an indication of a whippet's ability or its character. Conformation should come before colour if you are after a working dog. Unless you are set on a certain colour, have an open mind. Apart from in the show ring, a flashily marked whippet will have no advantage in the field. Whippets come in all sorts of colours, and combinations of colours. Personally I'm not a fan of brindles in the kennel but I do like them in the field, especially the lighter fawn brindles. Nothing else blends quite so well into the dried bracken and grasses where we do a lot of our work around here. Blues are better than blacks in my opinion in terms of camouflage.

It is of vital importance that you take on your puppy at the right time. Too young and he will miss out on vital socialisation with his mother and litter-mates, too old and he will lack the ability to adjust to the human world. While weaning can be done relatively early puppies aren't ready to leave their litter-mates until they are at least eight weeks old. These first two months are vital, not only for a dog's physical development but also for their mental welfare. The hurly burly of life among a litter is a vital part of a dog's learning process. He learns how to play, what is too rough, what and where the boundaries are. In short, he learns to be a dog. If a puppy can be too young, he or she can also be too old. After they have learnt to be a dog, the puppy has to learn his place in a human world. For that he needs one-on-one time with people, with children, with new places and new situations so he is easily able to adjust to everything life will throw at him.

It is absolutely vital that your puppy has been, and will continue to be, well socialized. Between four and eight weeks of age the puppy learns the vital skills of interacting with his litter-mates. Watch any group of puppies at play and you will soon realise that there are many different ways dogs communicate with each other. They use an impressive repertoire of signals, eye contact, body postures and vocalisation. Even in play puppies are busy

Blues can blend very well into the background.

learning from each other and developing all the skills they will need later in their working life. Chasing, catching, wrestling, tumbling and holding their litter-mates are all ways of rehearsing how they will hunt and hold their quarry.

Through play and play fighting, he learns how to interact with other dogs. If he goes too far, even in play, a sharp nip from a litter-mate will soon put him right. The dam too will intervene if he pushes her too far. Even the most loving of dams will cheerfully growl and put a boisterous puppy quickly back into his place. A few weeks of this treatment will soon teach him the boundaries of acceptable canine behavior. And, after all, good manners when interacting with other members of their own species are a vital precursor to treating humans with confidence and respect. During these first few weeks it is also vital for puppies to have as much positive human contact as possible. So any puppy you buy should have had lots of opportunity to play and to interact with the wider world around them. A quick look around the breeder's set up and a few questions will soon let you know how well this aspect of rearing a litter has been carried out. In short the more a puppy can see, hear and experience in a safe environment, the better. Even very young puppies can absorb vast amounts of information and an early introduction to the business of life gives a puppy and his new owner a head start.

So what do you look for in an individual puppy? Healthy and happy are probably two of the best watchwords. The first is evident in a puppy with a bright, alert eye, whose coat is shining and smooth and who looks on the world and on you with interest and enthusiasm. Litters of thin, pot-bellied, dull-coated puppies should be avoided at all costs for these are symptoms of worm infestation and inadequate care. Teeth should be clean and arranged in a scissor bite, the upper ones protruding ever so slightly more and overlapping the lower ones. Ears should be clean and free of any discharge or swellings. Dew claws should have been removed cleanly with no remaining lumps or bumps to cause recurrent trouble later in the dog's life. Apart from the dew claws, the nails of the feet should all be intact and been regularly trimmed. Have a list of questions in your head, prepare them beforehand. Write them down if you have to. Take your time but don't take forever. Some things can be seen in an eight-week-old puppy, some can't.

Having finally made your pick, there are still a few things to be done before you hand over your hard-earned cash and wend your way homewards. Make sure you see and actually look at the parents' pedigrees. If there is anything that is unclear or you want explained, don't be afraid to ask. Most breeders will happily discuss their dogs and their ancestry, for hours if you let them. If your puppy is registered with the British Kennel Club as ideally it should be, make sure you get the relevant paperwork, and get it signed in the right place by the breeder. Like many institutions, the British Kennel Club has many failings but its registration system should guarantee that any puppy you buy will be a pure whippet and display all the characteristics you would expect of the breed in looks, temperament and behaviour.

Find out what they have been fed. And ask how often they have had their meals. If you can't get hold of the same make, ask the breeder for a small amount to take home with you. Every reputable breeder will be only too happy to oblige to make sure their puppy gets off to the very best of starts. Many will have already put some by for this very reason. Make a note of when they were last wormed and with what type of wormer.

When you pick up your new puppy go prepared, especially if you have a long journey ahead. A travelling crate is a good idea if you have one. Most puppies will curl up and sleep, feeling quite safe in this contained environ-

Whippets make wonderfully calm companions.

ment. Unfortunately, it cannot and will not stop them being sick, but at least it can contain the mess. If you or a member of your family can't bear to put the new, cute puppy in a travelling box then have plenty of newspapers, old blankets or towels to hand, for the comfort of the puppy if not for the sake of your car.

Get home as soon as you can, get your puppy settled in as soon as possible and then you can get started on getting to know each other, and beginning your life together.

2 THE EARLY DAYS

Training dogs and in particular training young dogs is all about creating the right habits, and the earlier you start, the quicker and easier this is. You are not asking anything hard, or demanding anything that doesn't come naturally to your dog. And you will be helped even more by the fact that dogs are social animals, they want and even need to work with a human partner.

When you get home, bear in mind that this is a whole new and very scary world for an eight-week-old puppy. Gone is the protective influence of his dam, gone are the comforts of being part of a litter. He will encounter new sights, sounds, smells, perhaps even mix with strange adult dogs. All this can be very intimidating for a young dog. You owe it to them to make the experience as easy as possible. Be prepared for your bold, bouncing puppy to have been almost magically transformed during your journey home into a cowering, slobbering wreck, frightened even of his shadow. Depending on the character of the puppy and how you handle the situation, this shy retiring phase rarely lasts long.

If your whippet is registered with the Kennel Club then he or she will already have a name. Depending on the imagination and the taste of the breeder this may or may not be to your liking. Either way, it is highly likely that it will be far too long-winded to be of any use to the working dog or his owner. So you will have to come up with something of your own. There may be times when you will have to bellow this out in front of total strangers or, worse still, in the hearing of good friends, so make sure it is not a name you will later regret using. And you could do far worse than to take a leaf out of the sheepdog handler and trainer's book. Their working collies are always given short, snappy titles that trip off the tongue easily and their pronunciation is always kept distinct from any commands to prevent confusion in the field.

Even when I intend to keep a whippet kennelled it will always begin its time with us in the house. These early months are invaluable for their socialisation. With the best will in the world, few of us have the time to spend hours playing with a puppy in the garden or kennel. Winter makes it a chore rather than the pleasure it should be. And besides, it does no harm to house-train a puppy. You never know whether or when you might want to bring him or her indoors. Perhaps they will be taken ill. Perhaps you want to whelp her first litter close to hand. Perhaps you will stay away. Like all training, the very process of teaching and learning helps to create a strong bond and understanding between dog and handler.

The best advice I can give anyone acquiring any new puppy, of any breed, is to invest in a metal dog crate. It is invaluable for house-training and provides a safe haven for the puppy. They are ugly but are invaluable when it comes to house-training a puppy quickly and with few accidents. However, resist temptation of putting pup in there every time he misbehaves/gets too boisterous. He needs to learn how to behave around people and in a household environment, and he's not going to learn very much shut in a cage.

If your dog is in the house, now is the time when house-training can start to take its toll. If you have children they have probably got bored of putting the new puppy outside every five minutes. You have all got fed up of mopping up the inevitable accidents but if you really want your whippet in the house, don't give up. Push through that pain barrier and know that the more attentive and consistent you are, the sooner these little accidents will be a thing of the very distant past. House-training really is quite simple after all. A puppy needs to relieve itself several times a day with the need being all the more acute after he has woken and following a meal. Don't let your puppy disappear out of your sight and don't give him the chance to get in trouble and pick up bad habits. Get a wire crate and use it whenever you can't give your full attention to the puppy. Most dogs hate soiling their own bed and you can use this innate cleanliness to your advantage. Just remember that puppies have small bladders and with the best will in the world they can't stay clean for long. Once they have learnt to dirty their crate, they can develop this into a habit. Once they lower their standards it can be hard to restore their initial cleanliness.

All puppies need, and like to chew things, usually things they are not supposed to. There is, however, a good reason for this. Like human babies who have an insatiable desire to put things in their mouth to chew, the dog's desire stems from the same reason: his teeth are fighting their way through his gums causing him a fair bit of discomfort. Milk teeth are just that, small puppy teeth designed only to see the dog through his early months. The sooner these are replaced the sooner he should settle down and stop seeing your favourite slippers as teething aids. But chewing can also become a habit, a bad one at that. Biting down not only helps dull the pain, it can speed the process of cutting his teeth and distract him from the discomfort of it all. Most dogs have all forty-two of their permanent teeth by the time they are seven months old. Even if you do your very best to keep such things out of reach, accidents will still happen.

When they do, do not despair, and certainly do not lose your temper. Treat it as a lesson in dog training, for you that is. One of the most crucial principles of training is timing. Punishment after the crime, even a few minutes later, is a waste of time. Worse, it does harm. The dog either associates his punishment with some other innocuous activity or merely begins to resent the inconsistency of his trainer. Too many people endow their dogs with human reasoning, even human emotions and it does their dogs no good at all. The well-known saying that it is better to be late than never, *never* applies to dog training. If your puppy can't be caught in the act, then there is *nothing* you can do but to let it go.

A puppy is going to chew. At teething time they simply cannot help themselves. True, some seem to develop a lasting habit but all will at some stage sink their teeth into some precious possession. Prevention of such a scenario is far better than the cure. Make sure remote controls, shoes, toys, handbags, all things valuable or precious are all put and kept well out of reach. Give your puppy bones to ease his irritated gums and have a store of chews or raw hides to keep him occupied.

And you can forget their innocent expression and apparently fragile appearance, whippets can be quite incorrigible thieves and amazingly acrobatic in their attempts to get at a particular culinary delicacy left on the side. Anything sweet is especially vulnerable. A box of chocolates wrapped up under the family Christmas tree one festive season fell prey to a visiting whippet. Even under a huge pile of presents they were sniffed out and he was found carefully, silently and ever so gently tearing shreds of wrapping paper from the corner to get to the goodies underneath. Sometimes whippets really do seem more feline than canine in their stealthy actions and playful antics.

While I urge understanding, I caution against spoiling. Whining should not be rewarded. While it may start up as a legitimate expression of loneliness, this doesn't last long. And there is no faster way to create a whining, whingeing whippet than to reward them for their vocal protests by letting them out of their crate/letting them sleep on the sofa. Decide in advance what the ground rules are, and stick to them. And make sure every other member of the family does so too. Be consistent. Don't let misplaced sympathy undermine your efforts to produce an obedient working dog and companion. Remember that what is cute in an eight-week-old puppy can be nothing short of maddening in an older dog. Keep in mind what you want: a working whippet to be proud of. So there can be no tugs of war with toys or dummies. There is no surer, or faster, way to a hard-mouthed dog of any breed.

If you have children then you will probably need to guard your puppy from too much rough and tumble. Puppies can be likened to human toddlers in many ways. For a start they think they can do a lot more than they are actually physically or mentally capable of. Put simply, a young puppy is no judge of what is good for him. That is your job. Fortunately your average dog takes a lot less time than a human to mature, although some whippets never seem to grasp the art of growing old gracefully. Watch out for steps and stairs. A young puppy's bones and joints are still developing and vulnerable to damage. Child stair guards are a useful way of sealing off dangerous climbs, and drops.

One boy and his dog.

Kennelling is very much an option with a whippet. Don't be misled by their slight appearance; they are tough characters and given dry, draught-proof accommodation, company to keep them occupied by day and keep them warm at night, they will be quite content. It would be rather unfair to thrust a whippet out in a kennel alone in the dead of winter but a healthy dog given the chance to acclimatise to our relatively mild British climate will be quite content with their lot. In fact, these slightly tougher conditions can actually be of benefit to a whippet destined for a working career. A kennelled dog will develop a denser coat than his house-kept counterpart which, with the benefit of central heating, will not need to develop such a covering. A good coat will stand him in good stead in wet, windy and cold conditions when any dog needs all the help he can get.

You, your family, and your new dog have survived the first few days. The initial excitement, and unavoidable stress, should be starting to die down. This is the time to think about settling into a routine and beginning a programme to turn your inexperienced and impressionable puppy into a healthy, happy, confident working companion. These first few months are among the most important in your dog's life. He will be growing up, mentally as well as physically, at a phenomenal rate. Now, although much of his time and effort will be taken up with this demanding process, there is also a huge amount you can do to shape his development in a way that will help you, and him, forge a lasting and successful working partnership.

The first few weeks are really quite an exciting time as your new puppy's character starts to emerge. Is he naturally shy and retiring or is he forward-going, bold and confident? Or, is he a mixture of both? These latter dogs can be the hardest of all to train. You'll get a good inkling but don't be too disappointed, or too pleased either if your pup appears to be overly timid or overly bold. As with children, nature has a lot to do with what you end up with, but nurture has an enormously important influence on this too. Parents, dog owners and trainers, we are all in positions of authority and responsibility. We owe it to our charge, canine as well as human, to do the best job we can to make their lives as good as they can be. A dog's character will continue to develop and you have the exciting opportunity to help shape this process.

You should have stocked up on whatever food your puppy's breeder has used. 'Whatever' doesn't mean any old dog food will do, however. In fact, I would be reluctant to buy a puppy from any breeder who has skimped on providing quality food for his puppy. If he has neglected to provide his growing litter with all the nutrients they need, where else has he or she cut corners? But obviously you won't have bought from such a breeder, at any price. So your puppy has been brought up so far on a good quality puppy food; now you have to keep it going. There are almost as many diets out there for dogs as there are for human beings. I use a proprietary brand of dried complete food. It is convenient, keeps well if properly stored, but most important of all, it has all the necessary vitamins, minerals and energy that a growing puppy needs. It has been formulated, researched, tried and tested by professionals with far greater resources, much more time and far more expertise than I could possibly ever acquire. Reputable manufacturers, by definition, have a reputation to protect and that relies on happy owners breeding, rearing and raising healthy dogs.

Using a proprietary brand gives me peace of mind but don't let me make your decisions for you. However you choose to feed your dog, if he looks fit and well, you're doing the right thing. When it comes to puppies and young dogs that are still growing, one thing is certain, they need the best and plenty of it. A vast amount of physical and mental development takes place in just a few months. His bones and internal organs, his muscles and his joints are all growing and strengthening. The internal organs are developing and his vitally important immune system is developing and dealing with all the world has to throw at a young dog's vulnerable body. The brain is growing, absorbing huge amounts of new information and making sense of hundreds of new experiences. All this activity requires energy and all this growth and development requires the right ingredients. A quick look at just what the growing puppy needs can help you decipher the nutritional information on the back of the many and varied dog foods on sale, and to choose the best for your dog.

First there is protein. It provides the building blocks for muscle, skin, coat, vital organs and all other tissues. Young puppies need a lot of this to fuel physical development. The minerals, calcium, and phosphorous are both vital for healthy bones and teeth. It gets a bit complicated here because these minerals don't just have to be in the mix, they have to be there in just the right ratios which I think is another very good reason for leaving it to the professionals. Omega fatty acids promote a healthy immune system and help keep the skin and coat healthy.

There are just a few more things to bear in mind when it comes to feeding young dogs. While bones are great for teething puppies, make sure they are of the right kind. Some bones, cooked or raw can potentially cause harm. Chicken, pork and fish bones can splinter all too easily and cause severe, even life-threatening intestinal damage by tearing the stomach lining. Clean water should always be available. If for some reason you have to change your puppy's food, do so gradually over a period of a couple of weeks. Add a little of your puppy's new food to what he is accustomed to, increasing the proportion of the new variety every day until he is able to eat the new food without any upset. You will soon know about it if you are rushing the process. His stools will be looser and he will feel and look a little lacklustre as his digestive system struggles to adjust to the change. A puppy is a growing machine and any check to his development should be avoided if at all possible.

Don't give your whippet puppy unearned treats and don't let anyone else either. Whippets have a terrible reputation for being fussy eaters. They certainly can be. But then so can any dog given the right, or rather the wrong, conditions. There is nothing wrong with a timely edible reward for your puppy but scraps from the table and daily titbits are a definite no-go area if you don't want your whippet starting to pick and choose what he will and won't eat. It is a good thing to see a bit of puppy fat in a young dog. It shows that all his growing needs are easily being met. But, and this applies particularly to house dogs, avoid feeding titbits and treats. Some get so spoilt with titbits that they turn their noses up at dog food refusing to do more than nibble a few biscuits. Now, I have never known a whippet starve itself to death but they do look positively underweight, too thin to work well and embarrassing even to take for a walk to the local park.

Up until now your puppy should have been kept relatively free of parasites and disease through fortnightly worming by the breeder, and by the puppies naturally acquiring the dam's immunity. It is now up to you to continue waging the battle against worm infestation and to protect your dog from some of the nasty diseases that are out there just waiting for a vulnerable dog to amble by.

Given how often we hear how important it is to worm dogs regularly, there are still a shocking number of dog owners and breeders out there who neglect this most basic and vital aspect of dog care. I have heard of many excuses why worming is neglected but there can only be two reasons: ignorance and/or wanton disregard for a dog's well being. The first we can tackle right here, right now. The second is unfortunately far harder to eradicate and I make no claim to have found the solution. So why is it so important to worm? I make no apology for attempting to give an answer to this in depth. Ignorance might be bliss but not as far as your dog's health and well-being are concerned. Plus there is an element of self-interest here too. Not only do some worms carry a health risk to us humans, but every ounce of goodness and energy they sap from our dogs is lost performance in the field. A sickly pet dog might be able to go about its daily routine without too much difficulty but a working dog needs to be in tip-top form to fulfil its function, and to fill the bag.

I am not a vet but over the years I have probably acquired more knowledge about parasites than is good for anyone. But, as the saying goes, know your enemy and that applies as much to parasites as it does to people. Now there are two main sorts of worm that the dog, and dog owner, needs to be aware of, and on their guard against. Firstly, there are roundworms.

Apologies to those who enjoy their pasta but the best way to describe these creatures is to compare them to thin strands of white spaghetti. It is important to be able to recognise the roundworm as this is one creature that has no redeeming features. They are capable of causing much distress and discomfort to infected dogs. They attach themselves to your dog's intestines and eat whatever floats on by. You can buy the best dog food in the world but if our friend the roundworm is in residence in any significant numbers, all you will end up with are some very fat worms and a very thin dog. Worse still, they can infect humans too. Children, like puppies are particularly at risk. Licked faces and hands are a common way in which roundworms are transmitted from host to human. But anyone is at risk if they encounter infected soil.

Then there are of course the tapeworms, grotesque creatures that can, in the favourable conditions of a dog's digestive tract, grow up to 20cm in length and do considerable harm in the process. By a complex arrangement of head, hooks and suckers, tapeworms attach themselves to the lining of the intestines absorbing nutrients to develop their flat, segmented body. As they grow, these sections break away and can be seen passed out in the faeces. What cannot be quite so easily seen is the countless number of worm eggs these pieces contain. Flea larvae, however, happily consume these tiny eggs and carry the seeds of a tapeworm with them when they turn into adult fleas. And when these irritating parasites are ingested by a dog during grooming, the whole sorry story can begin again. Fortunately, young puppies are rarely affected but if routine worming treatment is not practised then young dogs are particularly vulnerable to the effects of any worm burden. Once again, prevention is far, far better than any cure.

It is never too early to start good worming practice. The battle begins even before your puppy was born, for roundworms are ready, willing and more than able to migrate from the pregnant bitch into her unborn puppies. Your puppy should already have been wormed regularly by the breeder. It is now up to you to follow their example and to continue their good practice. You have a duty to the health of your new dog to keep up a regular worming programme with a good quality wormer. Write the dates when your puppy needs worming in bold letters on your calendar, underline it in your diary, do whatever it takes not to let things slip. Where parasites are concerned, prevention is far better than cure. If you give your puppy's development a knock in the early stages he may never be able to make up the lost ground and stunted growth.

Vaccinations are vital to protect the young puppy from diseases that could cause serious illness or even death. In the United Kingdom these include canine distemper, canine parvovirus, infectious canine hepatitis, leptospirosis and canine parainfluenza virus. The microscopic viruses and bacteria are responsible for these diseases and can cause damage and distress far in excess of their diminutive size. So although vaccinations are expensive they are always worth it. Take parvovirus, for example. It is a common cause of viral illness in dogs in the United Kingdom at the present time. It affects the very young and the very old more, and more severely, than healthy adult dogs. Its symptoms cause great distress and all too often death in the untreated puppy. These include a foul-smelling, foul-looking vomit and diarrhoea which will often be stained with blood. Unsurprisingly the affected dog will be extremely lethargic and will become seriously ill in a matter of hours.

The dam's milk should provide antibodies for about two weeks after weaning after which time the puppy's natural immunity will start to weaken. Different vets recommend different times to begin a course of vaccinations so seek advice from yours and remember it is far better to be safe than sorry. No dog should have his life and his working career cut short by a preventable disease. Now vaccines work by stimulating the puppy's body into producing its own antibodies but this can take some time. Until your puppy has completed his full course of vaccinations, it is a sensible precaution to keep him from coming into contact with other dogs or visiting places that dogs often frequent such as parks. Something people fail to appreciate is that even older, vaccinated dogs can *carry* disease, and so can dog owners and any of their belongings that have come into contact with infected material. Parvovirus can remain active for about six months and is resistant to most types of disinfectants.

So until you are safe in the knowledge that your dog is protected from at least some of the dangers that life has in store, spend your time nearer to home getting to know each other. The time will soon come when you can venture further afield. You will need to regulate how much exercise you allow your young puppy to take. Whilst you certainly shouldn't neglect any opportunity, once they are safely vaccinated, to take your puppy out and about with you, limit the physical exertions he undertakes. He is using up most of his energy growing and developing and this requires rest more than running. The more positive experiences he can be exposed to the better.

Now is the time to think about having your dog microchipped, or rather not to think, but just get it done. I would encourage all dog owners to take advantage of this relatively cheap, quick and easy operation, but urge the proud possessors of running dogs above all others to take advantage of latest technology. Running dogs are, by their very nature, likely to get lost. Imagine the scenario, you have permission in a new place, a little way from your usual stomping ground and the ground is well stocked with rabbits. Wonderful? Absolutely, until your dog disappears over that brow and starts hunting up. Now that is only one reason why you should do your utmost to discourage this highly irritating habit but even the most obedient of dogs can sometimes succumb to temptation. Before you, and he, know it, your dog has travelled a fair way and got himself well and truly confused. Most dogs, given time, will return to wherever they last saw you.

Waiting, and making a fair bit of noise, is usually your best bet. Sometimes, this doesn't work, or isn't possible. More often, your dog will be found looking very tired and not a bit sheepish by some well-meaning walker or neighbour. Most 'rescued' dogs get reported to the local police or council dog wardens (and these should be your first port of call. It is well worth entering their numbers on your mobile – it could save you time and worry hunting around for the phone book later on). Knowing your dog has been microchipped and duly registered with the central authority should give you a little more peace of mind. All those working with strays from the council to the police have access to microchip scanners and it is now standard practice to scan any dog that is found.

An even more sobering scenario is when your dog goes missing, not in the field, but from the kennel and garden. Sporting papers and magazines are full of reports of much loved, highly valued working dogs that have been stolen. There seems to be a ready and thriving market for running dogs and lurchers, and cases of dog theft are rapidly increasing. And while having your dog microchipped, and advertising the fact, might not prevent them being taken, it might just help find and identify them at a later date.

A microchip can be inserted into a puppy from the age of about five weeks. It is put in place by a specially designed needle and by specially trained people. In dogs, it is inserted into the fatty deposits between the shoulder blades. Unlike tattoos, that other permanent method of identifying your dog, microchips do not fade, cannot be removed or otherwise interfered with. Once in place the unique microchip number together with the dog owner's detail and key information about the dog itself will be logged into one of several national databases. A hand-held scanner passed over the site of the microchip is all it takes to retrieve this and reunite dogs and their owners that have been separated either by accident or design.

It is absolutely vital that you continue the process of socialisation at home and abroad Between the ages of eight and twelve weeks old, puppies are undergoing an intense and rapid developmental phase. They are learning how to be sociable with other dogs and with people. He will be in your care now and you can really start getting to know each other. What you must not do is to waste a golden opportunity to instil good habits. Often the only effort required on our part to prevent problems and teach good manners is just a little bit of thought. Take calling the dog to you for example. It takes a dog a short time to learn his name if you give plenty of fuss and praise every time he responds to you. This is something that most women seem to find easier to do than men. In these early days, women are often more effective and make faster progress than their male counterparts, being naturally blessed with a smaller and less intimidating physique and physical presence. Most women also have a higher-pitched, less resonant voice that quite literally strikes a chord with puppies. It is reassuring, interesting and encouraging to the sensitive ears of any young dog and this importance of voice and its tone should be remembered during later training.

Now is also a good time to nip the highly irritating habit of jumping up in the bud. It may be rather endearing to be greeted with the unbounded enthusiasm of a puppy bounding up to you and bouncing all around. It is not so much fun when your twelve-month-old whippet dog, runs straight through a muddy puddle and then jumps straight up at you. You might not mind the mud and the wet but the force of the blow might well leave you gasping for breath. No force is required to discourage a puppy jumping up at you. When he does, simply step back so that he falls to the floor. At first he will be merely a little confused, soon he will be downright disconcerted, then he will be positively reluctant to even try to jump up. Make sure everyone that encounters him in these early days follows the same rules and you will have made a good start along the road to producing a well-mannered, well-adjusted whippet.

You will also need to get your dog used to as many people, places and animals as you possibly can. Quite simply, the more you put in, the more you get out. Translated into whippet training, the more time you spend introducing your dog to the many and varied creatures he or she is likely to encounter, the better mannered they will be.

Remember at all times that puppies, like goldfish and small children, have a very limited attention span. Short and sweet should be your watchwords at all times and during all the dealings you have with your new puppy. All this activity, all this learning and growing takes its toll and something all puppies need lots of is sleep. Give them plenty of attention and as many experiences as you can but also give them time to rest and to make sense of the great wide world and his/her place in it. A young dog can even tire of playing and being played with. Without time out and a refuge to escape to (another reason why it is a good idea to have a secure dog crate) a puppy can become as snappy and grumpy as the most short-tempered human being. And these are not traits you want to encourage.

While your puppy is doing his bit by growing up, you can start to assemble some of the equipment that will come in useful later on in training. It is not expensive and it is certainly not complicated or hard to come by. I recommend investing in a couple of retrieving canvas dummies and a packet of tennis balls. One of those hand-held ball-throwers that every dog owner in the land seems to own now is actually a very useful training tool as you begin to develop your dog's retrieving ability and his fitness levels, and when he steps up to the challenge. For teaching a dog of any breed to walk well and walk easily on the lead, then a choke lead as used by gundog trainers is the very thing. Put on correctly it immediately rewards the dog for walking to heel by instantly releasing the pressure on his neck. Great care should be taken to make sure that it is actually put on in the right way or it will not run freely and loosen when your dog is trying his best to please.

Remember in these early days to enjoy your new puppy. Look forward to your future together in the field and make a start putting in place the habits and behaviour that will make your partnership one to be remembered. But let him or her be a puppy too. Let them play and enjoy growing and developing. Whippets love to play, with other dogs, with you. In fact, their love of life and carefree abandon is one of the joys of sharing your life with a whippet.

All the tools of the trade.

3 THE BASICS OF TRAINING

The basic principles of training are simple. Make it easy for the dog to do right, reward him when he does and understand fully when to reprimand his transgressions and when to ignore them. There is a difference between discipline and punishment and the successful dog trainer never forgets the difference. Discipline is ongoing, consistent and clear. It gives you, and your dog, confidence and stability. That is not to say punishment should never be used, but it should never be used to teach a dog anything. It doesn't work. It is no good punishing a dog for a behaviour he doesn't know is wrong. All you will end up with is a cowering wreck or a stubborn brute, neither of which are much fun to be around, let alone work with on a regular basis. You don't punish mistakes, only deliberately bad behaviour. Be prepared to give your dog benefit of the doubt. Experience and observation will help you determine where the boundaries are.

Some people sigh with boredom whenever they hear the word obedience. I have even heard it argued, very unconvincingly I might add, that running dogs and lurchers not only do not need any obedience training, but that it hinders their performance in the field. Now, to me, that makes no sense whatsoever. A well-trained and obedient dog is a far more relaxed and content animal, and a far more relaxing one to have around.

Although a puppy in the first few months of its life is too immature for training proper to begin, instilling basic obedience can be done almost by sleight of hand at a relatively young age. Take sitting for example. By using feeding time to get your puppy's attention and reward his compliance with your wishes, you are teaching him and he is learning, all without either of you realising it. Do the same, but outside, and with distractions. But always do it away from other dogs. Even if they too know the game and can be relied upon to sit until given a command, your puppy's attention will inevitably be on them, not you. And that is not what you want at all.

With just a little thought, patience and planning many lessons can be integrated into your and your dog's life. Take feeding time, for example. Puppies and young dogs need relatively frequent feeds. While some people choose to leave food down at all times, I rarely do this. These early days are perfect, not for formal training but informal conditioning and for this you need to use every method and opportunity at your disposal. Food is the most important of these.

So you have a new puppy or young dog that needs three small meals every day. You can approach this in different ways. First, you can plonk your dog's dish down elbowing him out of the way while you do so and then get back to watching television. Or, you can use these as fantastic opportunities to teach your puppy some of his first lessons in manners and obedience. It is essential to demand and expect eye contact with your puppy. For a dog to obey a command he has first to look at his handler. This comes from gentle encouragement from you and the gradual development of respect in and from your dog.

To encourage him to sit, first hold the feed bowl above his head. As he finds it easier to sit and look up rather than stand, this is exactly what he will do. All you have to do is give the command 'sit' at the same time. Put the feed bowl down immediately. Hey presto, your puppy learns to sit instantly without ever being forced, only being rewarded. You repeat this process and you will soon find that your dog is not only responding to the command to 'sit' but he is also anticipating it. This is when you know that your dog has not only learnt his lesson; he has absorbed it with his mind as well as his body. It really is very simple.

These will probably be the only times in the early days when you will have your puppy's complete and undivided attention. Put any other dogs away. Get other people out of the room. Turn off the radio and the television. You, and the bowl of food, should be the only items of interest in the room or kennel. All you have to do is stand still. Ignore the excited antics of a playful pup. Don't even say anything. Just take your time and hold the bowl out slightly ahead of you. At first it might take some time for your puppy to cotton on, depending on his temperament, appetite and intelligence. But at some point even the liveliest puppy will take a break from cavorting around the place to look up at you and try to figure out what this new game is. You've won. Put down the food straight away and the first lesson is learnt. Keep this up until you receive instant attention and ideally eye contact the second you pick up a bowl. Now you can be a little more demanding. Not only does your puppy have to stay still before he receives his reward and his breakfast/lunch/dinner. Now we want him to sit first and to get him to do this without having to lay so much as a finger on him. Force gives him something to fight against mentally as well as physically and we want a dog that doesn't even consider resisting, let alone attempt it. And this begins at the very beginning.

When you call your dog you want and need him to respond immediately. Admittedly, with the best will in the world no running dog worth his salt will abandon the chase if he is pursuing a rabbit in full flight. But at all other times and in all other circumstances instant response is achievable and nothing less should be accepted. This level of obedience begins when he is a young puppy. When you call him, be inviting, get down to his level so you are not intimidating, make encouraging noises and when he does respond, reward him. Praise him, play with him; give him your total and undivided attention. Do this every time in the early days and your dog will associate the sound of his name and returning to you with all these pleasurable things. But remember if you do call him, insist he comes to you. The world is full of exciting things and all puppies are all too easily distracted. If you have to go and get your puppy, do it. Don't be lazy about this part of his training. You want to do more during these early days than teach your dog; you want to condition him to do the right thing at the right time, for the rest of his life.

This can be achieved and it isn't difficult if you put the time and thought in. It is never too soon to start your puppy retrieving just so long as you go about it in the right way, in the spirit of play rather than strict training. The aim is to instil the habit of retrieving straight to hand with no fuss and no hesitation. You want the whole process to be slick and to be quick. There are two very important lessons to remember at all times: always end on a high note and keep things very short and very sweet. At the end of your sessions your dog should still be eager and happy, his tail should be up and you should almost be able to see a spring in his step. It all helps to make him all the keener and more enthusiastic the next time.

Now there are a few little tips that will make these early days that little bit easier and will help get the two of you off to a flying start. Sit between your dog's retrieve and his bed; even better sit in his bed itself. That is where he will want to take his 'catch'. If you are there and if you take the time to make a big fuss of him, he will learn to love sharing it with you. Don't be too hasty in taking it away but also don't let him mouth it too much. Snatching it from him can all too easily encourage him to spit out his retrieve, the last thing you want the catcher of live game to do. If a dog has learnt, or been allowed to, mouth his retrieves he can develop a hard mouth, put in ribs and bruise flesh, hardly what you want your pot-filling dog to produce for you.

Get your puppy used to the feel of the lead. The easiest way to do this for both of you is to put a collar on your puppy for a couple of weeks before you try him with a lead. This way he will get used to the unfamiliar and unsettling sensation of something around his neck. Most puppies will walk quite willingly on the lead after this. I always keep the quick release slip leads just for working. It is all too easy for the catch to get caught and to release your dog in the most unsuitable places. Instead for training use either a collar and lead or a slip leash of the type used by most gundog trainers and

Rimrock Star at sixteen weeks showing keeness to retrieve.

A perfect delivery.

handlers. Most puppies will put up a fight worthy of the strongest salmon the first time they feel the lead around their neck. Be gentle and give him time to settle. Don't expect or try to make him walk smartly to heel. The time for that will come much later. All you want to achieve in these early lessons is for your puppy to accept the restriction of a lead and even to associate it with all things pleasurable. Stroke him, speak kindly to him. As soon as he shows the slightest sign of relaxing, take the lead off. Keep these early lessons short and keep the two of you happy and your progress will be rapid.

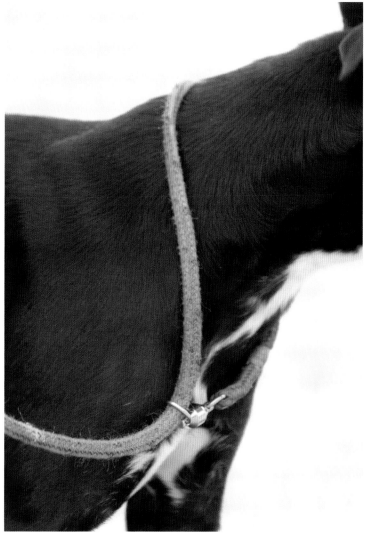

A lead, correctly worn.

Get him used to travelling. Take him for journeys in the car but make sure it is enjoyable as well as educational. When you go out, make a short trip and take him to a field or some open space and give him a run round at the other end. Make it fun, but make him behave too. An unrestrained and excited dog bouncing around a vehicle is not only a nuisance to other passengers but a danger to them as well as other road users. If you have a lot of dogs a purpose-made dog box for the back of the car is probably the most practical, if priciest option. Of course, if you are a bit handy with your hands (which I am not) you'll be able to knock something together. It doesn't have to be pretty (unless you want it to be) but it does have to be well ventilated, secure and big enough for the number of dogs being carried together at any one time.

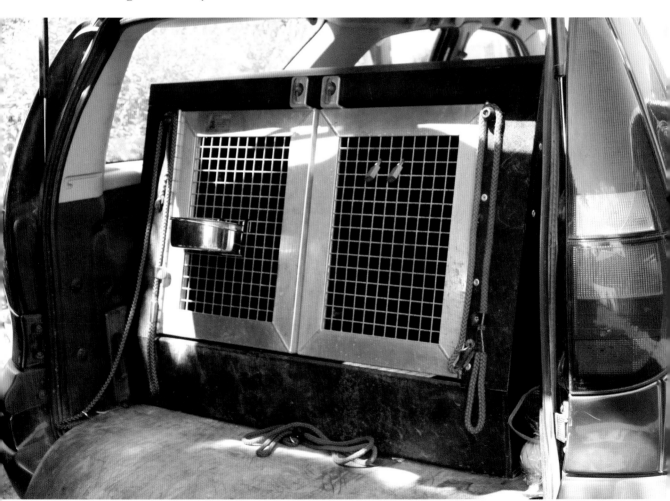

A purpose-built dog box is a wise investment.

If you do not have the time, the inclination or the ability to embark upon such an ambitious project, then there are many companies out there ready, willing and able to do the job for you. Some are more expensive and more elaborate than others. Some will fit into nearly all make and model of vehicle, others can only be carried in large estate cars and 4x4s. Take time to do your research, shop around, get some quotes and listen to recommendations. Better still, have a look at some in action. Looked after, a dog box will last you many, many years and will quickly become an invaluable and surprisingly personal piece of kit.

It is always safest for dogs to travel in a specially designed carrier. The only other option I would ever countenance, for one dog, or possibly two is to let your dog travel in the foot-well of the passenger seat. Whippets are such neat little dogs that they can curl up quite comfortably under the legs of all but the largest of passengers. Whippets are also the only working dogs I would ever travel loose. My car is far from clean but I do draw the line at soaking wet, smelly spaniels jumping all over the seats. Whippets on the other hand with their wonderfully short coats dry quickly and leave little trace even on the wettest day and after the muddiest outing.

Once again the key to having a dog that will reliably stay put neither distracting the driver or annoying the passenger, is to start their training young, more importantly to start as you mean to go on. Put your puppy in the foot well and tell him clearly to stay. When he tries to move, which he almost certainly will, simply repeat the command and firmly put him back into place. How long this battle of wills goes on will depend on the character of the individual dog concerned and how far he has progressed in his general obedience training. Once he understands what you want, and is prepared to stay in place while the car is stationary, and you are in it, then you can test him a little more. Get out of the car and watch his reaction. Almost certainly he will try and follow you over the driver's seat. Put him back and try again. And again. Stay patient and be persistent and he will understand what is expected. Obviously never leave him for more than a few minutes at most. To do so would be to try his patience too much, or worse, make him fearful of being left alone in vehicles.

Next you can try a short trip. Obviously, you will travel as a passenger until your dog understands what behaviour is expected in a moving vehicle. A vocal reprimand can also be issued when you see him shifting a little and thinking about moving from his allocated spot. As with most aspects of training, if you are clear and above all consistent, it won't take long before your dog understands and accepts his own special place in a vehicle. When you do take him out, always do so from the passenger door. It may seem unnecessarily time-consuming to walk around the car to let your whippet out but if he is never allowed to follow you over the driver's seat, he should never be tempted to break past you, putting himself and others, in danger.

Whippets can't help chasing. This trait can be seen even in old dogs that will give low-flying birds a quick chase and will happily catch moths and flies. Getting your dog used to, and accepting of, all the birds and animals he will encounter during his life is absolutely vital. Now is the time to take advantage of a puppy or young dog's natural timidity. It may sound just a little cruel but now is the time to introduce your dog to some of the animals and birds he will encounter, when he will be naturally afraid. Some animals are more intimidating than others, usually this is the male of the species but for sheer ferocity, nothing can rival a female protecting her young against any threat whether real or perceived. Be it cow, sheep, horse or hen; never put your dog in a position where he cannot escape. That really is cruel and is often counter-productive.

Ferrets will feature prominently in your dog's working life so introducing them is a good place to start. Get your young whippet used to them now and you will save yourself a lot of hard work, worry and embarrassment later. Anyone who devotes much time to rabbiting will understand just how precious a good ferret can be, not in monetary terms but in providing consistently good sport even in the most unpromising locations. Such a companion is truly invaluable and not one whose life and limb you want to put at risk. In the heat of the moment it is all too easy for a ferret to be snatched up by a keen dog. At best you'll have a whippet with a bloody lip and a very disgruntled ferret to pacify. At worst your ferret will be dead and your dog well on its way to developing a hard mouth, the last thing you want or need in a rabbiting dog.

The sooner you start this the better. Ideally you should set about it when your whippet is too young to do any damage, or even think about it. The gentlest nip or the smallest scratch inflicted on an impressionable eight-week-old puppy can make a lasting impression and guarantee a lifetime of healthy respect for their working companions. Feeding time again provides a golden opportunity for introducing new things and teaching new lessons. Allow them to share a bowl. Let them play together on the lawn. Ferrets, even the most seasoned and experienced workers, are always full of fun and will enjoy this time as much as a young puppy. Take care, however, with your choice of ferret for this and never let the pair of them out of your sight. Some ferrets can be very feisty and give a young puppy more than a gentle nip and do some serious damage, even permanent blindness if he bites near the eye.

And just because your whippet doesn't mind cuddling up with his familiar pal Freddy who lives in the hutch at the bottom of the garden, don't make the mistake of assuming he'll be equally at ease with your mate's polecat hob. When I say get your dog used to ferrets, I mean get him used to lots of them, white ones, polecats, silvers, small jills and massive hobs. He needs to be so used to the sight, sound and smell of these creatures that they become part of the landscape.

When it comes to what other animals your dog should be broken to, put a bit of thought in. Most rabbiting is done on agricultural land, but not all agricultural land is the same, ranging from arable to livestock and a mix of the two. In some parts of the country one or other system predominates. Here in rural west Wales, it is all livestock farming, mostly sheep with a fair amount of cattle around and about as well. Arable dominates elsewhere and it might be argued that those who live amongst vast fields of crops have a slightly easier time of it. If your dog is unlikely ever to encounter anything more mobile than a grain of corn swaying in the wind, it is less important they are thoroughly and well broken to stock of all sorts However, I am of the firm opinion that you should do your best to prepare for all eventualities. You never know what you might encounter in the countryside and, when you are fortunate enough to be allowed the freedom of someone else's land, it is doubly important that you can rely on your dog at all times. And where livestock is thin on the ground, you have to work an awful lot harder to achieve this.

The effort will be more than worth the time and trouble. It means peace of mind for you, and means you can give heartfelt assurance to any landowner that your whippet will not cause any damage to his stock. While strange dogs crossing land always cause some stress to any animals that are grazing there, a well-behaved dog causes far less disturbance and upset than others.

Word travels fast among farmers; do a good job and your reputation will stand you in good stead. But if you and your dogs behave badly, acres of prime hunting land will be lost to you forever, and deservedly so. Livestock are nothing less than a farmer and his family's living. With a well-behaved whippet you may find yourself welcomed on land that no lurcher has ever been allowed to course. Although able to give a hare a good run for its money (in the days when this was legal of course) the whippet is far less threatening in appearance than your average bull greyhound or other large lurcher.

Sheep should get a prominent place in any mention of stock-breaking. Almost all dogs will be tempted to chase sheep and it is a short step from chasing to biting and from biting to killing. Fully fledged sheep worrying leads to one thing and one thing alone: the destruction of the dog responsible. Sheep, with their woolly fleeces and skittish behaviour are enough to drive even the most sedentary dog to give chase. The sooner you teach your whippet that such behaviour is totally unacceptable, the better and easier it will be for both of you. Make sure your puppy is securely held on a lead before you venture close to any sheep. He should be sharply reprimanded for any interest he shows. Depending on your dog's nature and your response to his actions, he should gradually learn that he is to ignore any sheep he encounters. If you have access to or can persuade an understanding farmer to have access to his fields and shed during the spring lambing season, so much the better. A ewe with a lamb by her side to protect is a far different proposition from a flighty sheep. She will stand her ground, stamp her foot and even butt any overly inquisitive dog with her head. Such a response is usually more than enough to teach a young puppy that there is far more to the sheep than at first meets his eye.

Rams are another proposition altogether and most are capable and some are more than willing to chase any dog that ventures into their field and space. And the first thing a dog that is being seriously chased will do, is to flee to his handler and take cover behind him. The ram is no respecter of persons and you may well find yourself in the path of a powerful charge. As many rams are large enough to cause serious injury to the unfortunate human that gets in his way, the best thing you can do is to steer well clear of any fields containing rams for your safety as well as your dog's.

It is also worth noting and remembering that some upland sheep seem to have a smell that is peculiarly their own, and highly exciting to many dogs. Even bird dogs such as pointers and setters who spend their working lives quartering moorland sometimes succumb to the desire to chase these animals. Just think how much more tempting this scent must be to the innocent whippet. It is just something to be aware of and to be just that little more careful when in such surroundings. Never let your guard down completely when your dog is around unfamiliar stock and he will not go too far wrong.

Cattle are more likely to be encountered during the summer months. In winter when most rabbiting work gets done most cows are safely indoors to conserve the land. Given their size they are far less enticing to your whippet but a group of flighty steers can tempt the keen dog to get involved in the fun. Again, when your puppy is young, show him cows and calves if you can but also show him that any interest in them is unwanted. While your puppy is young and for the rest of his life if at all possible, keep away from cows and especially keep away from cows with calves. We are all familiar with the signs and the warning to 'Beware of the bull'. Most of us need no encouragement to steer clear from these obviously powerful and often aggressive animals but the greatest danger comes not from the male of the species. In the case of cows, the female really is more deadly than the male especially when she has a calf at foot. More walkers are killed in the United Kingdom by the strong maternal instincts of these animals than any other. Be warned and be aware.

Poultry is often to be encountered in and around many farmyards so your dog will also be able to take all these feathered creatures in his stride as well. The best way to get a dog accustomed to chickens and ducks is to have a handful wandering about on his home turf. This is possible even in the smallest of spaces and is the quickest and easiest way to condition your whippet to their presence and to teach him that they are facts of life not objects of fun. But if poultry keeping is not possible or practical then find somewhere with a plentiful supply of domesticated fowl wandering about and walk your dog on a lead among them as often as possible. A local park with a pond is a good place to start. Any ducks that live there will be more than used to strange dogs and will show a haughty disdain for any dog that comes close. Nothing will crush the eager enthusiasm of a young puppy to give chase faster than a bird or animals that refuses to join in the game by running away.

Horses are increasingly popular and either being ridden or running loose are all too often encountered in the countryside. These can be tricky animals to read. Their reaction to dogs ranges from abject fear and panic to vicious aggression. Steer clear at all costs and if you happen upon anyone riding put your dog on a lead and keep him away. Scared horses are dangerous things and those riding them are at serious risk of injury. Show respect and courtesy for other users of the countryside and they will return the favour.

Closer to home, whether you happen to have one of your own or not, your whippet will, at some point, come across a cat. If not well broken to them, he will easily chase and kill them. Whoever said that you are either a cat lover or dog lover probably got it right. I have never been able to understand the appeal of a creature that is clearly convinced of its superiority. This clearly also riles your average whippet who will happily inflict a fair bit of damage on any foolish feline. But I am also prepared to acknowledge that other people are besotted by their feline companions. You have the responsibility that your dog does not inflict injury, or worse, on anybody's precious pet. Introduce him to cats when he is young and he will come off worst in any altercation, and he will develop a lifelong respect for the teeth and claws of even the tamest cat.

Your dog should also have manners around other canines. Reared and properly socialised with his litter-mates and well disciplined by his dam, he should have an inbuilt and enduring ability to interact with other members of his species. However, although whippets are not by nature fighters and scrappers, there are exceptional individuals who have an attitude worthy of the most argumentative of teenagers. These will need more discipline and supervision but all whippets should look to you as the leader of their pack and not descend to squabbling amongst themselves.

They should give strange dogs wherever they are encountered a fairly wide berth but you should put them on a lead if and when you do encounter other dogs on your wanderings. Footpaths criss-cross the British Isles and with the recent 'Right to Roam' legislation that opens up huge tracts of land to the wandering public, you can never be sure that you will not encounter strange dogs and keen ramblers even in the most remote and unexpected of places. Be polite, be proud of your sport and keep yourself and your dog under the strictest of control and then you will have nothing to be reproached for and you will have been good ambassadors for all field sports and a fine example of a true countryman, or countrywoman.

4 Developing Your Dog

Now is the time to up the stakes just a little. With some solid foundations put in place you can start raising the bar just that little bit higher. Don't be afraid to take a step or two back and always be guided by your dog's reaction. The rules here are fairly simple. Make things fun and make sure they stay that way. Training can and should be enjoyable for all concerned. Taking your time at the outset pays dividends later. Take care of your dog mentally and physically and he should be fit enough to last you several good years in the field. Yes, there will be frustrating and tricky moments. There will be times when one step forward is all too rapidly followed by two steps back. Keep a smile on your face, or a grimace if it is more appropriate, and a sense of humour about it all. It is supposed to be enjoyable, remember.

This is when dangers of getting more than one puppy of similar age can become apparent. As they develop into dogs, one will always catch the eye, and take more attention than the other. We may start with the best of intentions but as the fate of so many well-meant New Year's Resolutions testifies, even the best-laid plans all too often go awry. For example, one puppy shows an early interest in retrieving. So what do you do? Following the above advice, you let the dog dictate the pace of training and on you go storming ahead of his slightly shier playmate. And the more time you devote to the one and the better he gets, the worse the other seems in comparison, and the less time and attention you spare him.

It becomes the most vicious of vicious circles. The puppy who needs the most encouragement fails to receive it while his precocious playmate takes up all the time. And indeed it is only natural to wish to spend time with the animal that rewards you the most for all your labour. And there is really little more rewarding than a dog that responds well to his lessons, and remembers them too. The tragedy is that there is absolutely nothing wrong with his less advanced companion that time and training wouldn't put out. Some dogs are naturally more reserved and reticent than others but if correctly socialised almost all can have whatever innate and natural talent they possess, brought out. In short, while healthy competition is good, comparison is bad.

It never hurts to give your dog his retrieve back. It works wonders with a dog that shows reluctance to retrieve right into hand.

Now it's time to make everything bigger and better, to ask and expect more from your whippet and from yourself. But without wishing to repeat myself, I must reiterate that it is of vital importance that when demanding more we do it slowly; it is far better to make haste slowly than to rush the job of training and preparation and push a dog to do anything before he is ready.

Returning at a good gallop.

I am ceaselessly amazed at the number of adverts I read in the classified sections of the sporting press for six-month-old lurchers 'catching on the lamp' or 'working well'. At this age they are neither physically nor mentally fit enough for the rigours of the chase.

On second thoughts, may be I shouldn't be surprised, for it is these very dogs who have been entered and worked far too early that never fulfil their potential and sadly never seem to find the permanent home they deserve. It is an easy trap to fall into, and a very tempting one especially with whippets who from an early age seem to show an amazing turn of speed, and ability to turn. Many can't wait to see their new speed demon behind a rabbit. Most will regret their impatience.

And besides, there is still so much preparation that can and should be done that there is no time to be bored with your progress. Take a picture of your dog at six months, make a mental note of his abilities and attitude to life at the same time, then compare it to the same animal at twelve to four-teen months old. He will be harder, faster, tougher in every way and far more mature in outlook. In short he will obviously be ready to work in comparison to the gangly younger specimen. This will convince you better than any words of mine of the wisdom of waiting. As the old saying goes: 'good things come to those who wait'.

So what does this preparation entail exactly? Well, it will be tailored to your particular needs but the fundamentals are the same. You are guiding your dog as he grows up, shaping him in mind as well as body to be the working companion that does his job and that does it well. In short, you are developing all the qualities of a good dog, one that you can justifiably be proud of.

Many dog trainers stress that training should only commence when a dog is six months old. They are half right, a young puppy needs lots of fun, lots of rest and plenty of relaxation. But that doesn't preclude introducing some gentle instruction into their daily routine. If done well training and socialisation are one and the same thing. There is so much that can be done before anything formal or demanding is started.

The process of getting horses used to the hurly burly of life is called 'bomb-proofing'. You should do the same with dogs, although the effects of neglecting this stage of training are less dramatic and dangerous in dogs than in horses which are liable to cart their rider off down a busy road and straight under the wheels of a passing lorry if not well and truly habituated to all manner of obstacles and given the confidence to face new encounters without panicking. Canines too can suffer and show symptoms of fear when this aspect of their training and education has been neglected. Dogs can become withdrawn, unable and unwilling to relate to the world around them. Worse still, any dog persistently in fear of new circumstances and encountering new environments will never be able to work to his full ability. He will not be able to focus on the task in hand. He will be far too busy recovering from whatever trauma he has recently experienced and permanently fearful of the next.

Perhaps every dog owner should follow the lead of the Guide Dogs for The Blind Association. As the world's largest breeder and trainer of working dogs they have learnt a thing or two over the years about what it takes to train dogs well. Not only are their dogs bred for their intended purpose – to help and guide their owners through the physical obstacles they will encounter throughout their life – they also undergo a rigorous period of training and preparation. Tellingly, it begins when they are at the tender age of about two months old when special puppy walkers take them into their homes and introduce them to as many sights, smells and sounds as they can. The more they experience and the more challenges they are able to over-come the better they will be at handling all life throws at them and helping their owners through it.

So what sort of things can we expect of our young whippet now? Let's say he is now about six months old. In many ways he is still a puppy, but we should now start to see more than the odd glimpse of the dog he will become both in his physical appearance and in his attitude to life in general and to training in particular. This is where people go wrong. Good intentions are abandoned. Caution is thrown merrily to the wind, and the consequences are rarely pretty.

You can start to be just a bit more demanding in all things. Your dog should be sitting when told. We have already established how easy this is to achieve by utilising feed times and your puppy's youthful desire to please. He can now be asked to remain in the sit position for longer. I don't use the command to 'stay'. If your dog has been taught that when he is told to sit he is to do so until you release him from the command, telling him to 'stay' will have no effect other than to confuse the issue. He should be able, eventually, to sit when told, and to stay sitting until released from this command, whether he can see you or not. When you are setting nets on a warren or scanning the countryside, you want your dog to stay put when you need him to. Now, not many whippets will stay calmly sitting when a rabbit bolts under their nose, and neither would I want or expect them to, but they should all stay still when confronted with the normal distractions and temptations of a day in the field.

How do you get this level of obedience? Well it began way back when your whippet was just a little puppy and you asked him to sit for his food. Without thinking, without being aware, he was being conditioned to sit whenever he heard the command to do so. If you have been consistent in your approach (and this is why it is so important that this is one intention and resolution that you stick to) your dog should not even consider that he has any option but to sit. That, of course, is the ideal and I doubt if there are any dogs out there (like children) who do not at some stage test the boundaries and try to challenge authority. Either way, when you are near him and you tell him to sit, that is exactly what he should do. No fuss, no hesitation, just sit and wait. Eye contact is good, head up waiting for you to decide what to do.

Now step back a pace or two. What happens? Most dogs will, feeling insecure without your immediate presence, try to follow you. That isn't what you want. The lesson you are teaching is that when told to sit your dog does so, freeing you to go about your business without a whippet for a shadow. Be gentle but be firm. You want the dog to sit *exactly* where you told him to, and when you told him to do so. After all, if you can't get him to do what you tell him within the confines of your own garden, what hope have you got in the face of all the distractions of the field? So put him back where he moved from, and try again. Patience is the key here. Slowly increase the distance. Circle around, stop, change direction, turn your back. Read the paper. You want your dog to be able to relax but also ready to respond. Nothing is more exhausting to man or animal than nervous tension. You need your dog to conserve all his energy for the chase.

When you can rely on him this far, it is time to be just a little bit sneaky: and use a bit of human intelligence to convince your dog of your god-like status. A garden shed is a perfect tool for this. Sit your dog up on the lawn and step inside. Make sure you can see him through a window, and that he can't see you. When he moves, and even the most obedient dog will move just a little, even if it is only to shift his weight or look around, give him a gruff growl. If he physically moves, get out there and as at the beginning of his training, put him back *exactly* where he was told to sit.

Never, ever in these early stages call your dog to you from the sit position. In fact, never be tempted to do this until he is absolutely reliable on the sit command, until you are one hundred per cent sure that he understands to sit and stay. Calling him to you before the lesson is fully leant and totally ingrained will only encourage him to move from the sit position in anticipation of you calling him to you. Dogs like this are a pain and likely to look to you at all times rather than pay attention to what is going on around them which is what you want in your ferreting dog. It is possible to cure a dog that has developed the habit of coming to you prematurely but it takes time, patience and a willingness to go right back to the basics and spend twice as long on them.

He should by now be used to and have accepted the feel and contact of the lead. He should be taught to walk willingly to heel, usually on the left of the handler, on and then off the lead. It never ceases to amaze me how many

Rimrock puppy demonstrating a gentle delivery at four months old.

*Use your imagination. Here a wall on one side and a leg on the other mean
your puppy has to walk smartly to heel.*

neglect this important piece of training. How much easier a dog is to work with when it will walk willingly alongside you, neither pulling ahead nor lagging behind. Off the lead it is far easier to control dogs trained to walk with you. How do we set about this? First of all you put your slip leash on properly with the ring on the lower side of the neck so it can run freely and release the pressure as soon as your dog responds. Then we find a suitable barrier that will encourage your dog to walk in the right place, at your heel. A wall or garden hedge is ideal for this. Keep your dog between you and the barrier and he will not be able to drift away from your side. You will have to ensure that he does not pull or walk too far ahead. This is where using a slip leash is invaluable as it does most of the training for you. It resists only when and only as much as your dog does. Being intelligent animals, dogs are quick to respond to this and as long as you keep your short periods of training up, you will soon have a dog that walks neatly to heel on the lead.

But we want to take it further. We want a whippet that will walk reliably at heel when off the lead too. We get to this in several small stages. We get the dog used to walking to heel smartly on the lead and to be mentally as well as physically with his handler by making frequent changes of pace and direction. If you keep him guessing you keep him thinking and paying attention to you. Should he deliberately pull ahead then a single sharp tug and firm reprimand is far more effective and far kinder than constant nagging. When we are sure the dog understands what is expected of him when he is told to 'heel', then we can let go of the lead and lay it along his back. The purpose of this is that he should not realise that he is free and should continue to walk willingly and correctly. If he suffers a lapse of concentration, as he is almost certain to do at some point, then the lead is there within easy reach and we can correct him with a sharp tug without any delay. The next stage is to loop the lead around his neck. Again he should be unaware that anything has changed but can be easily corrected if he should go wrong. When he is totally reliable at this stage then we can remove the lead from around his neck altogether. We won't dispense with it quite yet though. Drape it over your dog's neck and down the side furthest away from you. This is just a gentle physical reminder that you are still in control at a time when he will no longer have the restraining sensation of a lead around his neck.

The prevention of problems is so much better, and easier, than the cure. Don't just let your dog race away the second his lead is removed. Make him sit and wait for the command to be released. Vary the time you take over this too. Keep him guessing, and don't let him forget that all good things in life come from and through you, his trainer, handler and working companion. But perhaps your dog has developed this habit already. Don't despair. There are ways to tackle the problem that again rely on brains beating brawn.

What you need for this are a couple of leashes. Put them both on your dog but keep the second secret, one looped very loosely so it cannot be felt. Keep a firm pressure on the first until you remove it. When your dog tries to bolt away, he will be rudely and effectively checked by the second. You may need to repeat this a few times before you break an ingrained habit but it will work and you will win this battle at least.

Many dogs associate the removal of the lead with instant freedom and soon acquire the very annoying habit of sprinting off the second you take the lead off. Obviously not a problem if the two of you are out alone on acres of wide open space but unfortunately not all of us are blessed with such a place and space to exercise our dogs. In enclosed spaces, near roads, other walkers etc., such uncontrolled enthusiasm for their exercise can lead to disaster. Whippets are capable of travelling at great speed and regularly do so, just for the sheer joy of it. Allowing your dog to run uncontrolled is an act of irresponsibility, and a possible danger to your own dog, other dogs and other people as well.

And while we are on the subject of uncontrollable exuberance, here is a word of warning. At some point your dog is likely to refuse to come back to you when called. He might be deliberately disobeying you, swept away by excitement, or just not trained. All dogs should come back as soon as they are called. If this is not firmly instilled you are well on the way to losing control. And a dog that is not totally under control has no place on other people's land and amongst their stock. Nothing will give you and others seeking permission to hunt rabbits a bad name faster. You owe it, not only to yourself and your dog, but also to your sport, to ensure you are never guilty of this crime.

So what do you do when that day finally arrives, when your hitherto obedient and loving buddy hightails it across the field and out of sight, totally disregarding your calls and shouts. First, you must not do the very thing that, out of anger and frustration, you most want to do. And that is to greet your dog's eventual return with a torrent of abuse, shouts and other such displays of your displeasure. The ability of a whippet to take a rabbit at full stretch is second to none, but their ability to follow human reasoning is sadly lacking. Look at the situation from your dog's point of view. He has disobeyed you, and not only has he got away with it, he has had a positively good time doing so hunting up cover and having a jolly good sprint around the district.

You must never greet a dog that has disobeyed you and run off with a reprimand when he does return. You may have to grit your teeth to do it but when your dog does come back, make a fuss of him, praise and reward him. Put your lead on by all means but don't drag him straight back to the car and take him home. Give him another chance to have his freedom even if it is only for a few seconds. Even better, do this a few times before you head for home. He needs to know that coming back to you does not just mean lead on and straight home. Content yourself with the knowledge that although this particular battle has been lost, the war is far from lost or even over. In his mind he is being punished, not for the act of running away, but for returning at all. It is all too easy to see how a single small misdemeanour can rapidly turn into an insurmountable problem. Always try to see things from your dog's point of view. It is a far more straightforward one than our own. We are supposed to be the more intelligent part of the partnership. Training our dog is our chance to prove it. There will come plenty of opportunities in the field behind a rabbit for your dog to display his natural ability and prowess.

Now is also the time to step up your retrieving training. But do it in short sessions and always end your sessions on a good note with both you and your dog wanting more. You'll both be all the keener next time. Let's make a start with what we shall term memory retrieves. This is a technique more commonly used by gundog trainers but all dog owners and trainers can learn something from each other and this is a very useful tool. Now you might question why an owner of a whippet should want to employ this particular technique. Allow me to explain. It is a fantastic exercise to develop mind and memory, body and fitness. Briefly, the process is as follows. Pop a tennis ball in your pocket, put the lead on your dog and take a stroll along a quiet lane or straight stretch of ground. When you have his full attention flip the ball out in front of his nose and to one side so he cannot reach it. Keep him walking smartly on for a few metres or so. Turn around to face the direction of the ball, take his lead off, face him toward the ball which should still be clearly visible to him and to you. Give him whatever command you use to tell him to fetch and if you have judged the distance and your dog correctly he should race straight back to his retrieve with little encouragement and be back with you with little fuss and no bother.

Gradually increase the distance and time between dropping the retrieve and asking your dog to fetch it for you. As your dog's ability improves, you can drop a ball off the length of one, two or even three fields back before sending your dog back to fetch it. Just watch your dog sprint out and sprint back. This is not thoughtless, mindless play; this is directed, driven energy. Similarly you can increase not only the distance but also the time between letting your dog see the retrieve and when you send him to fetch it for you. Some dogs show a natural aptitude for retrieving, marking and remembering, but even those who are not initially quite as quick on the uptake can with time and patience become quite remarkable retrievers. Poachers of old appreciated this and would hide their catch along their route so that if they were caught there would be no evidence of their nefarious activities to be

Rimrock Queenie cleanly retrieving a small dummy.

found. When they were confident the coast was clear their dog would be sent back for their haul. Obviously this is not a technique that will ever be used today but it is a very good way of developing your dog mentally as well as physically. Once again, it is up to you how much you put into your dog. But as with putting money in the bank, the more you put in, the more you have there to draw upon when you need it. The same applies to training dogs, the more time and effort you put in, the greater the reserves of ability, energy and loyalty there will be when you both need it. It all contributes to forging a formidable and successful partnership, one that should last for many years.

Now there are plenty of dog-training dummies on the market. Just take a stroll around any game fair and you will be spoilt for choice, from small puppy size half-pound canvas ones to large hare dummies. They are not hugely expensive but you can make your own deluxe model very easily. All you need is an empty washing-up liquid bottle, one of the circular ones. Half fill it with water. Cover it with an old (but clean) sock. Slip on a rabbit skin and there you have it. Being only half full of water your dog learns how to lift his retrieve in the middle and to balance an uneven and shifting weight in his mouth, something he will later have to do when he encounters live quarry. Just a word of caution, don't ever leave your dog with his dummy or anything that you use for retrieving training. This will not only ruin your dummies, but will teach and encourage your dog to mouth his retrieves, an ugly habit at best, and one that can lead to a hard mouth at worst.

Remember how gentle you were when he was a puppy? Well, just because your dog is now bigger and more boisterous, don't abandon your careful approach. Nothing stops a dog retrieving to hand as quickly as a handler that roughly snatches his catch from him. This is irritating when it is a dummy or a tennis ball; it is positively disastrous when we are talking rabbits. Dummies lie there waiting to be picked up; few rabbits are as willing to wait around for you. When he brings his retrieve to you, be it dummy or tennis ball, encourage him to lift his head to you, stroke him, praise him, make him want to look at you and be near. You are no threat; you are his partner in this rabbit-catching enterprise. He needs you as much as you need him.

There is a live and vigorous debate over whether you should allow, let alone teach your dog to jump fences and other obstacles, and if you decide to, how you should set about it. Start small: it is far better to be too easy than too hard. Success is the fastest way to build your pup's confidence. Some puppies show a natural and early inclination to jump, and these are usually the ones that clamber and scramble out of their whelping box first and within days are popping over it neatly. However, don't be tempted even if you have bought one of these natural hurdlers, to push them too high too

Any attempt to mouth the dummy should be firmly discouraged.

fast. Make sure the first jumps you ask him to tackle are secure and that he has no alternative but to jump them. There must be no temptation to scramble underneath the obstacle or temptation to run around it. It's not about height in these early days but about beginning the process, developing his confidence and teaching him that obstacles are there to be faced, not avoided or refused.

Put your puppy on one side and get yourself on the other. Be enthusiastic about the smallest effort he makes, reward him for a successful attempt and soon he'll be popping over this mini-jump without any bother or any hesitation. While he's doing this give him a command, we use 'get-over' for all our dogs from Labradors to spaniels to lurchers and whippets, to indicate, funnily enough, that they are to get over whatever obstacle they come across. What you want to do in these first stages is to build confidence and boldness. What you don't want to do is to make your jump any higher. Your pup might look physically capable of leaping four times this height but remember his joints and bones are still developing and can be all too easily damaged by impact on hard ground.

Start your jumping lessons in a small, enclosed space. And once he has mastered one type of obstacle, introduce him to others. There is nothing more frustrating than a dog you know will sail over fences pull up short when he meets a wall, just because he has never been taught to jump one before. Your dog will jump and he will retrieve. While this is all well and good, unfortunately it doesn't mean he will do both at the same time. Just because a dog will happily jump and merrily retrieve, he won't necessarily do both, or do both safely. It comes as quite a nasty shock to proud dog owners when their accomplished retrievers pull up short when they come to a tiny obstacle when they are carrying a retrieve, and you can hardly blame the inexperienced dog for his hesitation. After all what most whippets are carrying will be a live rabbit with every interest in staying that way. They can be quite an uneven and unbalancing weight to carry. Get your dog used to carrying a small, puppy dummy over small fences and build up gradually. Again, when you start anything new, like retrieving over obstacles, make life as easy as possible for the pair of you. Go back to a kennel doorway or even the hall-way in the house; make sure it is just you and him and the retrieve. With a bit of luck and patience your dog should never doubt his own ability to tackle any obstacle with a retrieve and carry this confidence into the field with him too. And remember to make sure that whatever he is asked to jump is secure. The last thing you want is for his 'fence' to collapse on him.

His exercise can be increased gradually. From a daily romp in the garden you can increase the time and distance he is expected to cover. When the pair of you are out and about make good use of the obstacles you encounter. There will be ditches to be crossed, muddy gateways to be got through,

Start small with a light tennis ball and an easy fence.

hedges to be scrambled through. Whippets are most certainly not water dogs and you would be hard pressed to get one to swim willingly. Nevertheless they can and should be expected to ford small rivers and streams. All these things are new to a young dog and he will have to learn how to tackle them all. For all obstacles, use the command 'over'. It will let your dog know whenever he hears the word to tackle whatever faces him with confidence and gusto.

The same principle applies to jumping. Make good use of every obstacle you encounter, just so long as it is safe. That means no loose stone walls or old sagging wire fences. There is nothing worse for a dog's confidence or, for that matter, his physical

A whippet should tackle water obstacles boldly.

well-being, than on landing being followed by an avalanche of loose stones. Loose wire fences are deadly. It is far safer for any dog to jump a high, tensioned piece of wire than to attempt a low-hanging loose length of wire. Barbed wire injuries can be horrific and cut short the working life of a dog or at the very least scar him for life.

Teach him patience in all things. Now he is getting older he can be asked and expected to wait until invited to do all sorts of things from eating to jumping in and out of vehicles. It not only helps reinforce obedience but encourages respect for you and attention to your wishes. Besides, basic manners do more than make your dog easier to live with, they also make him less likely to come to harm.

Patience is something you should expect of yourself too. By twelve months he should be muscling up nicely. His pads should be hardened off. Some of his excess puppy fat will be burned off naturally with this increased exercise and he will start to really look the part. But resist the inevitable temptation to work your dog too soon. The main cause of ruined dogs is impatient owners trying to enter them too young too fast. Having put so much work in don't be in a rush to waste it all in a moment of madness. The time will come soon enough when the two of you can wreak havoc on the local rabbits. Until then, make good use of the time. It isn't wasted time. Your dog is maturing, mentally as well as physically. You are getting to know each other. You are getting the lie of the land, quite literally, in some instances. Whippets despite being relatively small dogs can take a surprising amount of time to mature. And when a whippet is pushed too far too fast, they can soon become vocal. And there is nothing more annoying than a yapping running dog. If this happens to you then stop everything and be prepared to put things on hold just that little bit longer. The best things really do come to those who are prepared to wait.

Retrieving work can be made more challenging. Now is the time to move on from dummies to the real thing. Make sure the rabbits you use for these early retrieves are cold and stiff. A freshly dead animal is a floppy, slippery mouthful, most unlike the experience of carrying a live rabbit which will be rigid and solid. Now when I say cold, I do not mean frozen and just out of the freezer, what I mean is a rabbit that has been allowed to cool, preferably overnight and to cool and stiffen. The rabbit must also be in good shape. No badly shot or mangled road-kill will do. There should be no blood, no mud, just a fresh, clean, cold dead rabbit.

You can make your command, once firmly instilled, much quieter and more subtle. 'Sit' can be shortened to a barely audible hiss when your dog is close at hand or heel, perfect for when you are working a warren. In such situations, when silence really is golden, hand signals are even better. Gundog trainers often use an outstretched arm with flat palm to reinforce

With training whippets can easily clear fences.

This is what we are aiming for. Rimrock Queenie clearing her fences with ease.

the sit command. There is no reason why it should not be used with a whippet.

Ever considered using a whistle? They are not the preserve of the gundog handler or sheepdog trainer alone. They can be a very useful addition to your kit enabling you to control and handle your dog at greater distances far more quietly and often far more effectively. Once the basic commands are instilled, it is easy to introduce the whistle.

Now is also the time to decide clearly what you want your whippet to do. One of the many joys of owning this breed is its versatility. While they are the rabbiting dogs par excellence, they can and do take a wide variety of quarry from the hard-fighting rat to the elusive fox (when such a contest was legal of course). What they don't do so well is switch from one quarry to the next without taking a hard mouth with them. If you don't mind your rabbits returning with ribs put in and bruised flesh, then this shouldn't worry you too much. Personally I feel this is a waste of a good dog and a good meal. There are plenty of other dogs out there who will decimate your local rats without a word of encouragement. The whippet is to my mind a specialist rabbiting dog and I like to keep mine that way. What you do with your whippet, however, is up to you. It's no good crying over spilt milk, nor is there much point complaining your whippet has a hard mouth after he's spent the season on rats.

Remember that all this time your young whippet is developing in body and mind rapidly and relentlessly. He needs mental stimulation aplenty and plenty of opportunities to discover and test his physical capabilities. But he also needs time and rest enough to make sense of all these new experiences and to let his bones and muscles grow and strengthen. Keep his exercise periods controlled and make sure your puppy has as much rest as he gets running.

5 WORKING AT NIGHT

More running dogs and lurchers are ruined by entering too soon and too young than by anything else. If you keep that fact in your mind when deciding if it is the right time to start your dog you shouldn't go too far wrong. Every dog is certainly different but not until your whippet is around thirteen to fourteen months old should you start to contemplate entering your dog. Whippets take their time to mature mentally and physically, and you should give them the time and the freedom to do this without prematurely introducing the pressure of serious work.

Already I can hear cries of 'my dog was catching on the lamp before he/ she was eight months old'. Good on them. But were they still catching when they were eight years old? Without making the slightest sound? Are they still sound in limb? They were? Good for you. But you were the lucky one. Nine out of ten dogs and dog owners would not have been so fortunate. Their dogs would have started yapping, developed a hard mouth, suffered recurrent injuries, gone lame frequently, and all these avoidable pitfalls which are all too often the result of pushing a physically and mentally immature dog too soon too fast. Be patient. You have your dog for years to come and it is a shame to ruin what could well be a beautiful relationship for the sake of holding back just a few more weeks.

The surest way of entering any dog is on the lamp as long as you make sure the conditions are right for the job. Pick a dark, windy night when there is no moon to give your presence away and a good breeze to help muffle the sound of your approach. If there is a light drizzle falling, so much the better. It all helps get you and your dog as close as possible to any rabbits out. And after all, anything we can do to help even the odds against an animal with sense vastly more acute than our own, should be seized upon. For rabbits live by one motto, if in doubt, run.

It goes without saying, or rather it should, that you should pick your ground carefully. If at all possible, get yourself on land that is not often lamped. A daylight recce is vital, even on old familiar hunting grounds. Now is not the time to discover the farmer has parked up a set of old chain harrows in the middle of a field. Such things can and do happen, and it is up to you to make sure you never witness the horrendous damage that results from a whippet hitting such an obstacle at full speed. Few dogs survive such an impact, and those that do suffer severe and permanent damage. For the sake of a few hours checking your ground, you will have peace of mind and, more importantly, a dog that is in one piece at the end of the night.

Check your ground carefully for any hidden hazards.

The best fields are those where the grass is about four inches long. Rabbits will sit tighter where there is this little bit of extra height, and when they squat tighter, you can get closer. In fact, some sit so tight that not only can you walk right up on them but you also have to poke them out with your foot to get a run. Forget sporting chances in these early days. Healthy rabbits are equipped with enough sense and survival instincts to give a good account of themselves even in these conditions. What we want for the young and inexperienced dog is success, and we want it quickly.

Death traps for a whippet.

I am in no way condoning the practice of 'bagging' rabbits whereby they are trapped and then released on unfamiliar ground purely to provide a dog with an easy catch. In such conditions your dog will learn little. The unfortunate rabbit will not behave as other wild rabbits do. A dog that is repeatedly given these easy catches soon develops an inflated opinion of its own abilities and when really put to the test in really testing conditions is frequently unable to take the pressure. It has not learnt the wiles and tricks of the rabbit on its home ground. Such dogs are likely to have their confidence unduly knocked when out in the real world they fail to catch their quarry quite as easily. Indeed, they often behave just like novice dogs when finally put to the test.

Keep your kit to the very bare minimum. Anyone who has spent a lot of time out lamping will want to lug as little as they can around the midnight countryside, and they will know that in such circumstances, less really is more. You can take rabbits perfectly adequately, in fact, downright success-fully, with a well-built, robust and reliable battery pack and a connecting spotlight. When it comes to choosing your lamping equipment, always bear in mind you're going to be carrying it yourself and you could be out and about all night. So you need it to be as easy to use as possible and that means it needs to be as light as possible. Lamps are no problem in this regard but packing the most power into the smallest space and lightest weight is not the cheapest option. There is almost always a trade off between the weight of a battery and its power and length of life.

You will also need to use the proper leash for the job. There are many different designs on the market and each and every one of them has their supporters and detractors and all of them will have their tales to tell. They can be made from nylon or leather, be short or long, be singles or doubles. Look for well-made leads. If they are leather, check the stitching regularly and take care of the leather or it may well crack and snap at the worst possible moment. If you are out alone with one dog, as you should be in the early days, then the worst that will happen is a prematurely slipped dog and a frustratingly empty field. The very worst thing that can happen is a dog slipping its lead when another dog is already in hot pursuit of a rabbit. Your lead must be able to withstand the pressure the keen dog will put on the slip mechanism when it is denied a chase. This is the time when accidents all too easily happen. A whippet after a fleeing rabbit is a single-minded creature, a missile locked on to its target. He will have no time to notice, let alone avoid, another dog that appears unexpectedly on the scene. Serious injury and all too often instant death are the usual outcome from such high-speed, high-impact collisions. Slip leads are more than a convenience: they are a safety feature and should be assessed and handled as such.

Lamping equipment.

Clothes should be warm and they should be made of a material that makes as little noise as possible. A rabbit has highly developed powers of hearing and he will detect the rustle of clothing and even low voices from a surprisingly long distance. Picking the right weather conditions will help you a little. Taking into account the wind direction when you are walking up the field will help even more. Being a little bit clever can help you a lot.

Properly prepared and kitted out you and your whippet will be ready for the off. It helps if you get it into your head that entering your dog is about furthering its training rather than rabbit catching. Go out alone. You don't want friends and family along for the show. Leave your other dogs at home too. True, dogs do learn from each other but the disadvantages far outweigh the advantages as far as I'm concerned. The first few nights are all about giving your young dog experience, and giving him your full attention. There are many dangers in taking more than one dog out at night. Slip leads are not infallible, confusion is not unknown, and accidents can and do happen. Not many dogs get up after a collision. Apart from all this, the presence of another dog will almost certainly distract a young dog from what is going on around him, and that often includes squatting rabbits. Another dog can also make your youngster reluctant to bring his catch right in to you. Dogs, especially young inexperienced ones are often very proud of their catch and loath to bring them anywhere near another dog, however close they may be in the kennel. Many will respond to the presence of another dog by refusing to bring the retrieve right in to your hand or, more frustrating still, circling the handler just out of his reach. It's hard to say which behaviour is more irritating, or which does more to alert all the rabbits in the area to your presence.

Don't be too ambitious or too demanding. Be happy with two or three runs. And give him time to settle and get his breath back between runs. Dogs that are still blowing when slipped are likely to do themselves an injury, and certainly won't be helped to make another catch if they are at a disadvantage before they even start. Don't waste your time or your young dog's energy and enthusiasm on unpromising slips such as the rabbit sitting just yards away from the warren. Such animals can be caught but not very often, not easily and not by young inexperienced dogs.

If he catches, don't exhaust him. If he misses, don't dishearten him. There will be plenty more nights and plenty more rabbits. If, and when, your dog misses his quarry, and he surely will, use the chance to get your dog back straight away. The second the lamp goes off, he should be back by your side. If he isn't, and he probably won't be the first few times you try the exercise, get out there and get him back. Raise your voice, let him know in no uncertain terms that you want him back, and you want him back when you choose, not when he decides he has had enough. Hunting up at night is a frustrating habit and one guaranteed to ruin more nights' sport than anything else. So if you sacrifice a few runs and spoil the first few nights' sport just to make sure your dog never develops this fault, then it really is a small price to pay. The end result you're looking for is a dog that is by your side when you turn the lamp off, not off by himself hunting up this field and the next.

Another pitfall to avoid at all costs is not bothering to get your dog back between runs. In a well-stocked field it can be very tempting if your dog misses on one rabbit, to switch the lamp onto another one sitting out. However, neglecting to recall your dog and insist on him obeying, will soon result in a dog that is wedded to the highly irritating habit of hunting up. It is not such a huge leap from you deciding which he is to course, and him choosing his quarry, and coursing it wherever it takes him. In such a situation he is out of control and you are out of the picture. Not much of a reward for all your hard months of effort and expense.

It is important when the moment comes not to get carried away with the excitement of the occasion. There should be nothing different in your behaviour or your dog's from those early days of retriever training. His first instinct if all the foundations have been thoroughly put in place, should be to come straight back to you, rabbit in mouth, and deliver gently to hand. Don't snatch. Don't grab. And while there might be a little gentle mouthing as the dog gets used to the experience, this should be gently discouraged. If not instantly addressed such behaviour can become a habit, and this habit can lead to a hard mouth. Don't be tempted to move towards your dog when he brings you his retrieve, any such impatient behaviour on your part will only encourage a hesitant return in the future.

Now all this may seem like a lot of messing but it really is worth it. In life you really do reap what you sow and that applies to training and working with dogs. Take your time and don't be disheartened if it takes many outings before you achieve success. Expect things to go right, be ready and able to deal with things if they don't and above all enjoy it. When the rabbit is in your hand and your dog safely back by your side, then it is time to celebrate. The pair of you are well on your way to a successful and hopefully long-lasting partnership.

While many whippets take easily and naturally to the business of catching rabbits and putting them in the bag, there are always some dogs that take a little longer to get to grips with what their work is all about. A particularly frustrating trait is that of running the rabbit with apparent enthusiasm and even ease, yet failing to actually take hold of the rabbit. Dogs that do this will often turn their quarry and sometimes even bowl him over with a foot but refuse to strike. This can be a maddening habit but it is one that passes given enough time and plenty of experience. There is no miracle cure or speedy remedy. The owner of such a dog will just have to keep slipping his dog at rabbit after rabbit until realisation dawns and instead of playing chase, his dog starts playing catch, and doing so in earnest. Stick to lamping until you and your dog are confident in yourselves and in each other. This may only take one or two trips or it might take much longer but it is vital during these early days to keep things as simple and straightforward as possible.

Lamping generally has quite a bad press and many landowners are reluctant to allow men and lamps over their ground. Permission is often hard won and you owe it not only to the landowner and yourself to treat his ground and his stock with the respect they deserve. If there are any conditions on your access, stick to them. Some of the land we hunt on is grazed by pedigree cattle. The farmer is delighted we take care of his rabbits,

Rabbits come out at dusk.

just so long as we wait until his prize cattle are safely indoors. Sometimes this might mean missing some promising nights early in the season but for access to some of the best lamping ground in the area, this small request really is a price worth paying. Whatever happens and however well you get on with the farmer, don't be tempted to turn up with a group of your mates and their dogs. The last thing any landowner wants to be faced with is a van full of strangers turning up in his yard and spilling out a band of unruly dogs. Aside from being just a little presumptuous, you run the very real risk of losing your best ground to one of your erstwhile 'guests'. Even the best of friends can be just a little underhand as far as their sport is concerned.

Inquire whether there are any fields or any stock that are out of bounds. Nothing is guaranteed to lose you your permission and your reputation faster than causing injury and/or stress to a landowner's stock, whatever they might be. The same animals that accepted your presence calmly during the day might be terrified by your appearance with a lamp at night. Many domesticated animals have poor night vision and react correspondingly badly to anything strange or unexpected in their midst. Different animals react differently to men, dogs and lamps appearing at night. Horses are particularly prone to panic so take care not only in, but also around any fields where they are grazing. Fortunately, most valuable animals are kept indoors during the cold, wet winter months, but don't take that for granted and take great care around any livestock that you come across. There are sensitive times of year as well as sensitive animals. Lambing is one of the most important times in a sheep farmer's calendar. If he doesn't ask you to abandon your night-time activities during these precious few months then you are honoured and fortunate indeed.

Make it your business to know the boundaries of your permission, and stay on the right side of them, however well stocked the neighbouring fields may seem. And take it from me, they always appear to be teeming with rabbits. But just make it your mission to get yourself permission there too and the best and fastest way of doing this is by word of mouth and a farmer's recommendation.

Incidentally one of the many advantages to running whippets is the interest and admiration they almost invariably invite from landowners we approach. There is something about their elegance and grace that catches the eye and sets them, and you, apart from the usual suspects. Whereas most landowners view bull-greyhound crosses (unfairly as it happens) as actual or potential stock-killers and collie crosses as closet sheep worriers, the whippet really is in a class of its own. Few farmers can imagine these neat little dogs doing anything at all damaging and are more than happy to give you, or rather your whippet, permission to work his land where others have tried and failed repeatedly.

A quiet dog is a must. Nothing will bring a farmer forth from his fireside chair faster than the sound of a dog opening up. Also stay clear of the yard. Most farms have a dog or two loose about the place at night, most of whom are alert to the slightest sound or presence of strangers. The farmer might have welcomed you but his dogs don't know that and will usually reward his generosity and greet your presence with an almighty barrage of barking. A night of disturbed sleep might be enough to make him rethink giving his permission to an inconsiderate lamper and his dog. A quiet handler is almost as important but for another reason. Rabbits are always on the alert. Strange smells as well as unfamiliar sounds will all startle him and put him on his guard. Smoking as well as talking should be avoided if at all possible.

Rabbits are not the only animals to be active at night. Any man and his dog out and about by night should also take precautions against an untoward encounter with that powerful animal, the badger. For right or wrong, they are protected by the strong arm of the law and also by a vociferous band of animal activists and amateur crusaders. They need to be given a wide berth for safety as well as legal reasons. Badgers are tough, they are aggressive, their fighting abilities and agility are second to none and they have an armoury of personal weaponry that can tear a dog apart, and do serious damage to any human hand that tries to intervene. Fortunately these largely nocturnal and protected animals don't tend to interest the whippets as much as they seem to draw the attention of some larger lurchers. Nevertheless take care, for if you are suspected, let alone caught interfering with a badger or his sett in any way, even accidentally, then you run the very real risk of prosecution. From the very outset, discourage your dog from any contact with these deceptively cumbersome creatures and stay well clear of them yourself. Any form of contact with a badger is a risky business.

Always let the landowner know in advance if and when you expect to be out and about. A quick phone call can work wonders, as can the occasional 'brace' of rabbits left at the door. Treat your ground and all that you encounter there with respect. A landowner is under no obligation whatsoever to let a man and his dog wander over his land at the dead of night. He is allowing you this freedom to get his rabbits controlled. Do a good job and you will deserve his trust and even thanks. It has been estimated, how accurately and by whom I have no idea, that ten rabbits can consume as much as one sheep, and that rabbit diggings can undermine even such mighty embankments as those that lie alongside some of our railways, so the landowner is benefiting from the relationship too. The efficient lamper, professional in his approach at all times, deserves respect. You should take a pride in what you do and in how you do it.

6 THE DAY SHIFT

Taking rabbits by day is a slightly harder proposition in some ways, easier in others. For a start our quarry is more aware and on the alert for danger. We do not have the benefit of darkness to help conceal our approach. Rabbits tend to stay closer to their holes.

Working whippets by day is also easier in some ways because at least our field of vision is far greater than that allowed by the narrow beam of the lamp plus we can enlist further help in the shape of a ferret. Whippets can hunt up very effectively and can develop a very good nose to go with the job but if we want to take rabbits seriously, in every sense, we need to use the ferret and nets.

We can easily solve the problem with ferrets. Put them down, up pops a rabbit to be trapped neatly in nets or scooped up skilfully by a well-placed dog. Funny, how it rarely happens like that. For a start we need a good ferret or ferrets, and this is not as easy as some seem to assume. They are not treated with the respect they deserve or valued highly enough. Anyone who has lost a good ferret and struggled to find a worthy successor will sympathise. And even the best ferret will not perform his best if kept in poor conditions and handled roughly.

So having heeded the above advice, let us assume for simplicity's sake that you are the proud owner of a reliable ferret, free from the many and varied vices that careless rearing and handling can instil. Now you have to pick your warren. As your team becomes more experienced you can be less picky and indeed some of the reward comes from tackling a difficult bury.

Try only to have one novice in your team at a time. You need to be able to focus your attention on one animal alone if you are going to make these early experiences positive ones and help set them up for a successful career rabbiting. If valuable lessons are to be learnt from early mistakes you will need to be focused on the task in hand and able to take charge of any situation that arises.

Hearing can and should be used to great effect on a warren when out ferreting. You can follow the action and direction of movement underground

Firm but fair ferret handling.

by just watching your dog's ears move. With small twitches and cocking of the head, they will follow what is happening, and more importantly, will give you a good idea of what hole the rabbit is going to make his speedy exit from. Some argue that serious ferreting can only be done without dogs. What I think they mean is that serious ferreting can only be done without badly trained and controlled dogs. A busy dog rushing about the place, getting tangled in nets, causing a commotion, thrusting his or her head down every hole in sight, is a undoubtedly a liability and almost guaranteed to stop any self-respecting rabbit from bolting and turn them back to face the ferret. At best this makes the poor ferret's job an awful lot harder; at worst it leads to a kill-in and hours of wasted time and frustration digging out a sleeping ferret with a very full stomach.

Many humans are more of a liability than a well-trained dog. Even some self-proclaimed experts at the job chat away merrily far too loudly and far too close to their quarry's quarters. Not until they are right upon the warren do most of them stop talking or even bother to lower their voices; lots smoke, a habit not only bad for the health but also it immediately alerts any wildlife about to your presence and approach. Once on the warren they move about too much and with too much fuss. Instead take time to stand back and survey the scene. Even well-known long-established warrens can have modifications. New holes, hidden exits and entrances should be checked for and covered. Now, even the most thorough ferreters are liable to leave a hole without a net and even unwatched. Here a dog can be invaluable. They can follow the movement and if a rabbit exits from one of these unseen holes, he can and should be ready. A short dash and the rabbit is in the bag. They are also there to take the rabbit that slips the net, and to guard the hole that is temporarily without a net. A good dog can put a lot of rabbits in the bag that might otherwise have gone merrily on their way.

If your dog has been trained to sit and stay and can be trusted to do so, all aspects of fieldwork will not only be easier and more efficient but also far more enjoyable. Even if all your dog does on an outing is mark holes then you will have saved yourself time and a great deal of unnecessary frustration. When it comes to getting your dogs to mark holes where rabbits are in residence, the less you interfere the better. Your job is to get your dog out and about in rabbit country where there are plenty of holes for him to investigate. With a dog's incredible ability to detect and discriminate between scents, it will not take him very long in this sort of environment to show a marked preference for freshly used holes by lingering longer about them. Watch him carefully for dogs mark differently and you will need to learn your whippet's particular ways, but never, ever praise his interest. It is not only unnecessary but it is positively counter-productive. As far as your dog is concerned he is being praised for marking a hole, any hole. As a

A whippet will guard the hole while you get ready.

result this is what he will continue to do. By the time you realise that this is his game, false marking will have developed into a habit, and a hard one to break at that. Apart from being downright useful, what better company can there be on any ferreting trip than your loyal canine companion. They never get bored, question your judgement or laugh at your mishaps. They are the perfect accompaniment to any day.

If you go ferreting you will need purse nets, and you will need good ones. The main materials out of which most purse nets are made are hemp, and nylon. They have their advocates and their detractors and they have their advantages and disadvantages. Nylon nets are cheap but there is a reason for this. They tangle easily and are frustrating to use. Hemp is the traditional material and it has stood the test of time. It is strong, easy to use and, if well-cared for, long-lasting. There lies the rub, however, for hemp being an organic material is all too perishable. If not dried properly after use, hemp nets soon rot; if not hung up out of reach of rodents, they are soon chewed to pieces. Synthetic materials last without any special care or thought but they also last if they are forgotten on the field and they can be a dangerous and unsightly reminder of your visit. A forgotten hemp net by contrast soon disintegrates leaving nothing more damaging than a hole in your pocket when you find you have to buy a replacement net.

Make sure your nets are securely placed.

Giving the handler space to work.

Of course, no ferreter worthy of the name should ever forget his nets. Accidents do indeed happen, but they don't have to. Keep your nets rolled up with an elastic band. As you peg out your nets, put each elastic band around your wrist. When your ferret is out and you are certain there is nothing left to bolt, pick up your nets and replace the elastic bands. When your wrist is free from all encumbrances, you know all your nets are back safely in your bag. It may seem like a needless precaution to take but every warren requires different numbers of nets down and in the excitement of it all it is all too easy to forget where your nets are. It is, after all, much better to be safe rather than sorry.

When you are using nets to catch bolting rabbits, take all the time you need to make sure you cover each and every hole you can find. Even apparently unused ones can be used for emergency escapes when a ferret is pressing his attack. And make sure that each and every net is firmly secured with its peg. All of the hole should be completely covered by an evenly spread net. All leaves, twigs and undergrowth that might hinder it pursing is removed. Do this as quietly as possible while you are setting the nets so that the rabbits below ground are not discouraged from bolting. If there are any holes near your warren, even if they are apparently unused, net them. Should a rabbit manage to slip a net and evade a whippet, it might well make for a nearby hole and could finally be back-netted.

This is where all your patient training starts to pay dividends; this is when you feel very glad that you dedicated just a little time to teaching your dog that 'sit' means just that, sit and wait until they are released from the command by you, or by a bolting rabbit. During these early days be strict; insist your dog sits where you put him. In this position he will not acquire the bad habit of interfering with your carefully positioned nets. Over time and with the right experience he will soon learn the purpose of the exercise and will stand off of his own accord. From this vantage point he will be far better placed to take any rabbit slipping the net or that looks likely to do so. As time goes by you can be more lenient; when you know your dog under-stands the game, let him move if and when he wants. A whippet worth his salt will not take long to realise the link between the noises he is hearing and feeling through the earth, and catching rabbits. He will follow this underground activity more closely and with greater accuracy than any human. All you have to do is let him. Don't keep using the 'sit' command when he and you reach these dizzy heights; it won't be necessary, and worse still it will merely undermine the command, and your authority.

Nets aren't necessary to catch bolting rabbits. Ferreting with whippets alone is perfectly possible, intensely enjoyable and although not always as productive, the time saved not having to place and pick up nets usually means more warrens and more ground can be covered in less time. The guidelines for a successful trip are the same as for ferreting with nets although most whippets learn far faster the link between the ferret entering the hole and a rabbit bolting out, and learn to follow the subterranean sounds more closely than when they are also being worked with nets. Here you get to see two very different animals hunting in very different ways yet working together and relying on each other. The only downside to this set of circumstances is that you, the human, can feel not only excluded but positively redundant and surplus to requirements.

Some people argue that a dog that is allowed to hunt up by day is rendered useless for lamp work at night. This might be true if your dog is allowed and always has been, to do what he wants when he wants to. It would be quite unfair and unrealistic to expect such a dog to differentiate between work at night and work by day, and the difference between them. If you have no means of recall you have no way of educating him about this either. However, a dog that has been taught the recall and to obey it at all times, is a far different animal and to my mind a far more useful one. As noted above your first few outings at night might be cut short by the need to remind your dog of the importance of obedience, but once this initial sacrifice has been made, a dog can be expected to hunt up thoroughly and freely by day as well as refrain from doing so at night. Instilling and cultivating this versatility and reliability is, after all, what training is all about. Personally I cannot conceive of abandoning either mooching about by day or lamping at night. And with a bit of time, thought and training of my dogs, I never have to. Neither should anyone else.

Some of the most pleasant days hunting are spent just hunting up likely looking ground with whippets alone. True, without the aid of a ferret, there are many places that you might struggle to catch anything. In fact you might struggle to see anything at all. However there are places where rabbits seem to scorn subterranean life, except that is, for rearing their litters. Here a ferret will help little. But here is also where a good dog, keen to hunt and allowed to do so, will prove invaluable. One of the reasons why so many of us find rabbit-hunting so very addictive is its unpredictability: the ability of the quarry to appear almost anywhere and almost always without warning. The most unpromising piece of cover can hold a rabbit while an apparently attractive thicket will contain nothing. Every day is different and every outing teaches you and your dog something new. This is the freest form of hunting and one that reminds a whippet what his nose is for, and how good he is at using it.

As with most things in life, don't expect things to go according to plan on each and every outing. Certainly don't expect your dog to figure out what is going on straight away. He may be well trained, obedient, broken to ferrets etc. etc. but that doesn't mean he'll have figured out just what he is supposed

Once mastered, the whippet can easily handle a fully grown rabbit at full pace.

to do on his first outing. It will take a few missed rabbits, a few snatched nets even and certainly one or two reminders from you for him to mind his manners. Enthusiasm can get the better of even the most obedient dog. This should not be a cause of despair and disappointment, but instead a reminder that what training is about is not destroying your dog's drive and desire to hunt, but to harness and direct it. And that really is only to be expected from a working whippet bred for drive and hunting ability. Be consistent and insist that even in this new and very exciting situation, he listens to you. Only if he has the discipline to stay still and take in all that is going on around him will he be able to learn what he is to do, and how he is to do it.

Just as your first few outings at night may have been devoted to giving your dog the right experiences, so allow yourself and your young dog a few trips out in the day to find your feet. None of this is a waste of time, even if you do miss out on a few rabbits. Accept it as part of developing your dog's natural ability and cementing your partnership, and the whole thing becomes enjoyable for the pair of you.

How long before you begin to relax your attention around your dog and rely on him to use his own discretion? Well only you will be able to answer that question. It depends on many factors from how much experience you can give your dog, how much attention you devote to him, to the process of training itself and how fast he is to learn his lessons. By now you should know your dog and be able to read him and his reactions. You will see him grow in confidence and ability. It will be an organic and gradual process. It is so exciting when you discover that your gangly and inexperienced pup is turning into a reliable and trusted companion, able to understand what is expected of him, and to fulfil it.

A young dog will hold a rabbit anyway it can.

I promised to concentrate on the dog, its work and its preparation but I'm sure most readers will forgive me if I digress a little and spend some time on that fantastic little creature the ferret, without whom the rabbit's life would be a lot easier, and the work of those that pursue him into his underground kingdom, an awful lot harder.

The ferret is a member of the mustelid family, but a domesticated one. His relations include stoats, weasels, polecats, pine martens and badgers and he shares their strong hunting drive and killing instinct. How far the ferret has been domesticated is shown by the marked inability of most escaped ferrets to do well in the wild. In fact most soon meet an unhappy fate if they are not soon recovered. Starvation and predation soon take their toll in the harsh and unforgiving natural world.

At long last, the sight you have been waiting, and training, for.

The ferret through no fault of his own does not have a glorious past; his life and his work are not celebrated in works of art, he is not mentioned in diaries and records. But he has been around for hundreds if not thousands of years. To what can we attribute this deafening silence? Maybe it is because his work is done underground and largely out of sight. His tenacity and his courage go unseen and unfairly unrecorded.

Curiosity may have killed the cat but it is the very characteristic that makes the ferret such an efficient hunter. All other members of the mustelid family share the same exploratory instinct. Every hole they come across has to be investigated. It will come as little surprise that an animal that hunts mostly underground and in the dark, hunts mainly by following scents and listening out for sounds.

Plenty, perhaps most, ferret keepers have these animals purely as a means to an end and this is sadly evident in the way in which these undervalued creatures are kept. No animal can possibly perform its best when kept in damp, dark, dirty and cramped conditions. Just because ferrets work underground, it doesn't mean they want to live in permanent darkness. True, ferrets can bite but that doesn't make them vicious; only poor handling and rough treatment can do that.

Many myths abound about ferrets such as they need to be kept hungry to hunt well. This is absolute nonsense. All a hungry ferret wants to do is catch, kill and gorge on fresh flesh. And after this great feast, to curl up and go to sleep, heedless of his handler's impatient curses above ground. Getting this ferret back will take time and involve considerable digging where this is possible. Its well-fed, fit counterpart, however, wants to catch and kill too, but if he does manage the latter, he will be content with a small feed and will keep you waiting for minutes rather than hours. Ferrets that are fed flesh at home too are less inclined to eat themselves silly if and when they kill a rabbit underground. For these well-cared-for creatures there is nothing particularly exciting about a just-killed carcass and there is no desperate urge to fill their bellies.

In spite, or perhaps because of the want of care they have received over the years, ferrets are generally a hardy lot, not prone to disease and illness so long as some basic and very simple guidelines are followed. All ferrets should be kept clean, fed regularly on good quality meat and have constant access to clean drinking water. Jills, unless mated are prone to illness. If you don't wish to breed your own ferrets every year then it is worth securing the service of a vasectomised hob to keep your jills healthy as well as happy.

If you are on the look out for your first or even some replacement ferrets you need to make sure you are getting hold of the right sort. Some ferrets are better than others at their job and you would do well to source your own ferrets from parents who were excellent rather than just average workers.

The best ferrets tackle their work with enthusiasm and energy, never waste time, can be trusted to produce the goods, or rather the rabbit. Few ferrets, however, start off brilliant. Although endowed with great hunting instinct and drive, they nevertheless have to learn the finer points of working their quarry. Patience and experience are what is needed here to help them reach the peak of their abilities.

White, silver and even sandy coloured ferrets are often preferred over their polecat brethren. It is commonly believed and with some justification that their coat colour makes them easier to spot in dense undergrowth and cover. Plus white or light ones are thought to be much easier for your dog to identify and differentiate from bolting rabbits as well. Personally, I have no particular preference. The ferrets I have are silver and white but that is purely the result of chance not design, and if I was offered a polecat ferret that I knew to be a good worker, I would have it and work it like a shot. If the undergrowth is that thick, even a white ferret will be impossible to spot. Noise is the greatest give away. For small creatures, ferrets can't half make a racket above ground as they shuffle through dead leaves and small twigs.

Colour is a matter of personal choice but size is of far greater importance. Small really is beautiful as far as ferrets are concerned. Some of the larger hobs can be so heavy and cumbersome that if they get hold of a rabbit underground it has no hope of escape. Even if he wanted to the rabbit cannot bolt; it will be killed before it ever reaches the light. Small jills are able to slip through purse nets without disturbing them at all.

If you get a young one about August time this gives you a chance to get to know each other. Yes, I know it sounds a little daft but ferrets are quite sociable little creatures and do develop a familiarity and an affection for their owners provided they are treated with respect and kept with care. It is always better if possible to have more than one ferret. For such ferocious predators they love to play and love even more to play with each other. And it is really fun to watch the way ferrets play with complete abandon and total absorption.

It can be tempting to take on an older ferret especially if it is offered free. These, however, are the very last ones you should be willing to accept. If you have no choice, so be it, but be very wary about taking on an older ferret unless you have either seen it work or know the owner well, and know that he will not pass on rubbish, or better still both. As with most working animals when an adult ferret is put up for sale there is almost always something wrong with it, some flaw in its working ability.

It may have developed the highly irritating habit of skulking near the entrance to the hole, refusing to come out and retreating into the safety of the warren when approached. Hours can be wasted trying to persuade such a ferret to allow you to pick him up. It is little comfort at the time to realise that such behaviour is invariably the result of poor handling by human beings earlier in life. Nothing will make a ferret hand shy faster than being snatched at by fearful or impatient handlers.

Ferrets are on the whole the most tolerant of creatures; they have to be to survive the rough treatment and poor living conditions that are inflicted upon so many of them. Even people with the most immaculate of houses and gardens seem to exclude their ferrets from similar care. Ferrets have a reputation for being smelly. It would be more accurate and far fairer to say that too many owners of ferrets don't take enough care of their charges. For ferrets are really quite clean creatures and there is no excuse for not helping them keep their surroundings comfortable. They will use one area for their toilet so scraping this out regularly is the easiest and quickest of tasks, especially if their living accommodation has been well thought out and constructed.

They should have as much space as possible. They do not suffer from claustrophobia, their work after all is done below ground in the dark, often in cramped and confined spaces, but they need and benefit greatly from space to exercise and play. They work underground, but they do not spend their life there. True, they are able to curl up into the tightest of balls but, again, they don't want to spend their life like that. They are playful athletic creatures that need space to let off steam and keep themselves fit. Rabbit warrens can be huge and it is unfair to expect a weak and unhappy ferret to set about his work with any enthusiasm and zest, or to have the stamina to do a thorough job.

What all forms of housing must have is good ventilation but no persistent draughts. Their living quarters should be easy to access so that ferrets can be caught easily and cleaning out can be done quickly and with little effort. I am all for conserving energy and minimising the time that has to be spent on the boring jobs. They will need a separate sleeping compartment with plenty of dry warm nesting material. The whole thing should be dry and damp proof. Plus it needs to be out of direct sunlight as ferrets are very susceptible to heatstroke and dehydration from overheating.

In addition you will need a spare hutch or similar to house your jill and kits should you choose to breed. It is not impossible for jills that have been kept together for some time and even a well-hefted hob, to have and rear a litter of kits all while living under the same roof. It is possible, but not however to be recommended. Accidents can and do happen so if you want your kits to be safe, keep them separate.

It really is very simple to feed your ferrets well. They are completely carnivorous and need meat. If it is fresh and clean ferrets will eat pretty much any animal you offer them. You can keep ferrets alive and just about functioning on less nutritious helpings but young kits will definitely suffer as will a nursing jill. Gone, thank goodness, are the days of bread and milk slop. Feed whole carcasses as often as you can. Even the indigestible and inedible parts all have their part to play in keeping the ferret fit and well. The ferrets will pick and choose what they need and when to eat. Any surplus they will stow away. For this reason, be very careful with chicken especially if fed during the warm summer months. Gone-off chicken contains all manner of bugs and is capable of killing adult ferrets as well as wiping out whole litters of young kits. Road casualties can make good ferret food but only if they are fresh and you can be sure that they died on the road not as a result of poison. There will be times when you will have a glut of potential ferret food to hand so it makes sense to have a freezer dedicated solely to animal food.

It goes without saying, or should do, that your ferrets need a constant supply of fresh clean water. The best way of providing this is through one of those pet water drinkers that can be attached to the outside of the wire front and can be readily accessed and kept full. These little carnivores can get through a lot of water. Meat has a high salt content and ferrets will need to slake their thirst often.

There are plenty of ferrets out there but not all are good workers. Some seem to have sleep permanently on their mind, some like the easy life and will just take a quick tour of the warren following only the main burrows and producing only a fraction of the rabbits below ground. The good ferret by contrast will hunt out every square inch of tunnel, only being willing to be caught when the job is done. They may appear frequently but until they have flushed anything and everything there is to be found, they will be tricky to catch. So if you have good ferrets guard them jealously and keep your line going. You will regret it if you don't. In view of that, here are a few tips about breeding that you might find helpful. I am not an authority on ferrets, nor is this a book about them, but some basic information about breeding gained through personal experience might just be of use and/or interest.

If a jill ferret is not mated she will stay in season for many months. This relentless hormonal activity takes its toll on her health. They are vulnerable to some serious and potentially fatal diseases such as pyometra and metritis, and many, but not all by any means, actually die when left in this unmated state. If you have a jill, then come the breeding season, you will need to seriously think about this.

Mating is a noisy business, and looks very brutal. The hob will grab the jill by the neck before having his wicked way with her. It will be fairly obvious even to the most inexperienced ferret keeper when his jill is in season and ready to be mated. The vulva becomes swollen and turns a darker shade of pink. As soon as she has conceived, the swelling will go and the colour will fade away. As all this activity usually takes place in the spring

What could be better?

and early summer, there should be little temptation to work a pregnant jill. To do so is to risk injury and damage to the jill herself or her unborn kits. She will carry her offspring for six weeks before they are born into the world, tiny, blind, naked and totally helpless.

After about five weeks of gestation the pregnant jill will start to look the part. She will thicken considerably around her waist and if this is not her first litter, her teats may also begin to swell slightly. As the birth nears, the jill will begin to busy herself making a cosy nest. There must be plenty of fresh, dry nesting material near at hand and the box itself should be clean. Feed her as normal. An overweight ferret is as unhealthy, if not more so, than an underweight one. Leave her in peace as much as possible especially if she is young and inexperienced. An older seasoned campaigner might well tolerate a lot of interference but few jills are this tolerant and the unfortunate consequence of an upset jill is that she can turn into a cannibal at the slightest provocation.

You should also remember that even the quietest and ordinarily friendly jill can react with unusual ferocity to protect her litter. Mundane routine tasks such as cleaning out and feeding can become fraught with danger for the unwary handler. It is a small consolation to know that this is not a mistake you will make more than once.

The most surprising thing about a litter of newborn ferrets is their complete and utter helplessness. There can be hardly any wonder that things can and do go wrong when these vulnerable squeaking creatures are being mothered by a creature with such a highly developed and highly charged hunting instinct. They are tiny, totally naked and completely blind. However, their development is rapid and by the time they are about three weeks old they will have started feeding on meat brought into the nest. Not long after, their eyes begin to open and they begin to explore the world or rather the hutch around them. Start to handle the young ferrets as soon as you can. This is vitally important if you want tame non-biting ferrets.

If you have sensible children that can be trusted with the task now is the time to get them involved with the new arrivals. All young ferrets want to do is play and if handled gently and with respect they become tame rapidly. They respond rapidly to playful affection. Stroke them, tickle their tummies, pick them up, and carry them about the place. Get them used to as many sights and sounds as you can. On warm summer days get the whole litter out on the lawn but make sure you have enough eagle eyes fixed on the inquisitive youngsters. Ferret kits can quickly get themselves lost and into all sorts of trouble if an ever-watchful eye isn't kept on them.

Your ferrets may be happy at home and keen to work but first you have to get them to the field. I've seen hessian sacks in use. They are very cheap, if you can get hold of them in this era of plastic carriers and containers for

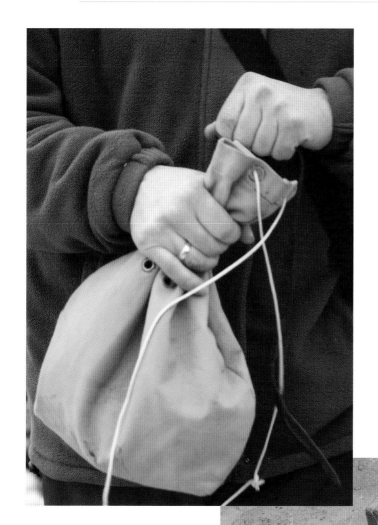

Carrying bags should be well secured.

everything, but they can be hard to keep secure. Plus they allow draughts through, they don't keep the rain and damp out and offer little in the way of protection for the inhabitants. Canvas sacks with air-holes are another option. They have a drawstring that can be securely tied and attached to your belt when you are out working, and some people swear by them. But when they are new the canvas can be quite stiff and, I imagine, fairly uncomfortable for the ferrets inside. I prefer carrying boxes with separate compartments for each ferret. I find multiple boxes can be a pain with all the ferrets making a bid for freedom at the same time. A well-made wooden box will keep the rain and the wind out as well as provide protection from dogs with more than curiosity on their mind. They might be just a little awkward to carry about the place but that is a small price to pay for peace of mind.

Ferrets should be no younger than five months old before they are taken out to work. They will need little training; in fact there is very little you can actually do to prepare your ferret for the field other than keeping him fit, healthy and willing to work with you. Don't expect miracles the first time you use a young ferret. They are naturally inquisitive and will enter and explore every hole and tunnel they come across, even if there are no rabbits at home. You may feel frustrated but don't show it. Handle your ferret gently whatever his early performance, or apparent lack of it. He needs time and experience to develop his confidence and working ability. It is up to you to provide both. A good marking dog will help enormously here and for the rest of his career. If your ferret has been well handled and well fed you have no reason to even consider using a line, or long piece of string, on your novice ferret.

When you are out and about adhering to some simple dos and don'ts can mean the difference between tremendous success and abject failure. Don't make a noise and don't smoke if you can possibly help it. Strange sounds and smells are almost guaranteed to keep rabbits underground and make it an awful lot more likely that your ferret will kill underground. It also increases the risk of injury to your faithful ferret. Rabbits are not helpless under attack. Just one kick from an adult rabbit's powerful hind leg can do serious damage. Even pet rabbits can terrify a small child. When a ferret emerges after being below ground for a long time take a good look at his claws for as often as not they will be clogged with the fur of the rabbit he has tried to dislodge from a dead end tunnel.

Don't ferret for rabbits during the warm summer months. Dense undergrowth will hide the entrance and exit holes of most warrens. The movements of ferrets above ground will be hard to see and they may be more easily lost. Most important of all the rabbit will be busy breeding. Nearly every warren will contain baby rabbits, easy pickings for any predator. So while your ferret is cheerfully munching his way through bite-size morsels of rabbit meat you will be cursing above ground. Knowing that you have only yourself to blame for your impatience, if not stupidity, will not improve your predicament. While you are cursing and digging, your ferret is diminishing the stocks available for your winter sport.

Your ferret needs to be fit to work well. For this reason he should never be starved. Even in these enlightened days, you can still come across people who firmly assert that to be an efficient hunter a ferret must be kept hungry and preferably be as vicious as possible. This is total nonsense. All you end up with if you keep them underweight is a ferret that kills underground and needs a lot of digging out.

And you cannot possible argue that a ferret cannot tell the difference between the human hand that has always handled him with care and the sight, sound, smell and feel of the rabbit which he has evolved over millennia to hunt. Ferrets don't have to be vicious to be good at their job. The worst thing you can do with ferrets is to be nervous around them and when handling them. Ferrets are like most animals, and most of us. Give them plenty of room, fresh air, exercise and good food and you can't go too far wrong.

7 THE RABBIT AND HIS WORLD

The best hunters love not only their quarry but the whole natural world around. They always strive to learn more and understand better the countryside that surrounds them. The rabbit may not be as fast as the hare but it more than makes up for this relative lack of speed with its agility, its ability to put in jinks, twists and turns, and to do so without checking its speed in the slightest. The rabbit is one of the most commonly seen British mammals but living in large numbers doesn't mean that they are easy to catch. Far from it.

Rabbits may not be as fast as a hare but they can still move at speed.

No book about the whippet could be considered complete without a closer look at the rabbit, the quarry to which it is peculiarly well suited and to whose pursuit many of us devote so much of our time, energy and effort.

The rabbit occupies a strange place in our common consciousness. It is officially classed as vermin, often hated by landowners and yet much sought after as quarry by a large number of people. Unlike pheasants, partridges and other game birds and animals, the rabbit is an animal that most landowners want rid of and many are happy to see controlled. It is one of those unusual animals, an edible quarry that isn't carefully guarded.

It has captured the imagination of many different people in very different places, and for many, many years. Even in the past there has never been a common consensus as to how the rabbit should be regarded. In ancient Aztec mythology there was a pantheon of four hundred rabbit gods whose debauched behaviour, unsurprisingly, represented fertility, parties and unbridled drunkenness. On another continent entirely, the Central African character, 'Kalulu' was a tricky customer, a rabbit that always got the better of bargains by fair means or, more often, by foul. Closer to home, in America and to a lesser extent in the British Isles, the rabbit's foot is associated with good luck and carried as an amulet or charm. This slightly gruesome practice apparently has its origins in the mysterious system of African–American magic known as 'hoodoo' or more popularly as voodoo. The mythical rabbit in Britain is probably most closely associated with fertility as embodied by our Easter bunny that makes his appearance at that time of rapid growth and renewal, the spring.

But the rabbit has other connotations too. On the Isle of Portland in Dorset, it was thought to be very unlucky to even speak its name, and for a very good reason too. Quarrying was the traditional industry, and some of its practices made it an exceptionally dangerous one at that. In order to save space, the mounds of waste stone, those which were for one reason or another unsuitable for sale, were built up and into high walls. These rough structures were vulnerable to the rabbit's own quarrying and tunnelling activities. Without warning these walls could and did collapse and could and did cause injury and death to any unfortunate miners in the vicinity.

But it is far from being considered a pest to those who hunt them. The location of good rabbiting ground is often a closely kept secret and permission to hunt there, jealously guarded. The relationship that so often develops between the pursuer and the pursued is one of respect, admiration and interest. Over the years a knowledge builds up through observation but it certainly helps speed the whole process up if you have just a bit of advance information.

It has long been accepted that the rabbit is not one of our 'truly' indigenous British species, although they have been firmly established here for quite some time. Thanks to recent archaeological discoveries, their status is not quite so clear. It was thought that rabbits were originally restricted to the Iberian Peninsula and to the north west of Africa, until the Romans conquered most of the known world around two thousand years ago, taking the rabbit along with them. Without doubt their range has extended, most likely as a result of human intervention. They have been introduced to many other regions either to provide food or for hunting, or most commonly of all, for both.

The exact time and place the rabbit first made its appearance on our British shores must for all intents and purposes be lost to history. For years the accepted wisdom has been that it was the Normans who brought it over the Channel after their conquest of England in the late eleventh century. Perhaps they did. They would most certainly have needed a ready and constant supply of good quality meat to feed the conquering troops and to supplement the diet of the new ruling aristocracy, but rabbits have been used for food for hundreds if not thousands of years. The Romans kept them in secure enclosures called *leporaria*. Archaeologists have discovered remains that suggest the innovative Romans brought this practice along with their legions to the British Isles. At an excavation at Lynford in Norfolk the two-thousand-year-old bones of a rabbit were uncovered. The cut marks on these bones indicate that it was butchered to eat.

This, however, is not the first rabbit to have lived in Britain, for archaeologists have also discovered the remains of rabbits that date back some five hundred thousand years, long before the Romans even existed. How can we square this circle? Well, we can't with any sort of certainty but archaeologists can give it their best guess and that is that, yes, the rabbit did happily inhabit our shores once upon a time. But then along came climate change and Ice Ages pushed the rabbit further down south. The only way it could make its way back to the lush grazing grounds of our island were with human invaders, first the Romans and then, more likely than not, the Normans.

The practice of keeping rabbits enclosed in specially built warrens is recorded in surviving illustrated manuscripts and written documents. These also record the existence of a special post of warrener, held by a man whose duties were principally to care for his rabbits and present them to the great households' kitchen staff. Some of these men must have been a bit lax in their care for enough rabbits managed to escape to breed in the wild and form not only a viable but a thriving wild population. In fact, so well did the rabbit take to its new environment that it rapidly became not an animal to be cared for and confined, but a detested pest and species of vermin.

As many as one hundred million rabbits were believed to be roaming the countryside and laying waste to the farmers' valuable crops. And this despite the many and varied natural predators that love to feast on rabbit flesh and the concerted efforts of man to control the rabbit population. At least it was a pest that when dead, skinned and dressed, could help to feed a hungry family. Up to and until the advent of that dreaded virus, myxomatosis, rabbit was a regular item on the menu. A shilling each was apparently the going rate at the outbreak of the Second World War.

The rabbit caused so much damage that it was included in 1954 Pests Act. This law imposed on landowners the responsibility to keep their ground clear of rabbits. The whole of England (apart from the City of London and the Isles of Scilly) were declared a rabbit clearance area. Today, rabbits are regarded by landowners, not as a source of income, but as a particularly resilient pest. And no wonder: their burrowing undermines hedgerows and weakens fence posts and their relentless scratching and digging and disturbance means only the hardiest plants can survive. Unfortunately, productive grass is not one of these. Weeds such as nettles and docks, thistles and the poisonous ragwort take advantage and take hold rapidly leaving little of nutritional value for a farmer's stock to munch on. It has been calculated, by whom I am not quite sure, that ten rabbits can eat as much as one sheep.

However, it is not just the amount they consume but the way they set about it. What grass that is left is eaten away by the resident rabbits or killed off by the accumulation of their droppings. Rabbit droppings and urine is decidedly acidic and can cause damage to ground and alter the balance of plants able to thrive. Prime, lush grass gives way to scrubby weed species of low fodder value.

Not only do rabbits graze the grass but they have a penchant for stripping trees, young and old, of their bark. New forestry plantations are surrounded by supposedly rabbit-proof fencing. It would be a very optimistic, or foolish, individual who planted any young trees anywhere without protecting them with special guards designed to prevent rabbit damage. A tree can survive a few nibbles but remove even the narrowest encircling strip of bark and the tree is doomed. And the sharp teeth of the rabbit can ring a young tree in a matter of minutes.

But the seeds of the rabbit's downfall could be found in their very success. When death and destruction came to them, it was not in the form of any natural predator but in the artificial introduction of a fatal and cruel disease, myxomatosis cuniculus, or as it is commonly known, 'myxi'. This viral infection arrived in Britain after a long and roundabout route around the globe.

It has a rather colourful history. A disease fatal to rabbits was first reported in South America way back in 1898. It was the Italian bacteriologist, Giuseppe Sanarelli, who gave this virus the name by which we know it today: myxomatosis.

It was first used as a weapon to be used against the rabbit population in Australia, being deliberately introduced as rabbits were proving to be a menace of unimaginable and unmanageable proportions. It was successful. Death and destruction followed the arrival of the virus in truly epic proportions. It seems highly likely that it was introduced deliberately to our own shores at the behest of landowners eager to be rid of their own rabbit problem. Since 1952 it has been illegal to spread disease in Britain using infected animals but an epidemic broke out in Kent in 1953.

Two weeks later it was recorded in Sussex, undoubtedly assisted by farmers and landowners keen to rid their land of what was widely regarded as a pest. Infected animals were carried and traded and soon the countryside was littered with dead and dying rabbits. By 1954 infected rabbits were appearing in every part of Britain – almost all the rabbit population of 60 million was wiped out. But the disease is no longer so lethal and the rabbit population is increasing again. Obviously, not all the rabbits would have succumbed or we would not still have these wild and wily creatures to hunt today. One in a hundred eluded the virus, bred and eventually helped to repopulate areas denuded of rabbits. It still rears its ugly head at regular intervals throughout the British Isles. But there are always some survivors able to repopulate areas as soon as the plague has passed on.

The symptoms of myxomatosis are particularly unpleasant and there can't be many country dwellers who haven't witnessed the suffering of the infected rabbits. The virus is carried by fleas that live on the rabbit and transfer the virus by biting new victims. The first sign that a rabbit has been infected with the virus is a watery discharge from the inflamed tear ducts in the eye. Soon the eyelids themselves begin to swell and in a matter of a few short days, the rabbit's eyes are sealed shut almost certainly forever. A pus-like substance fills these unsightly swellings which then appear around the rabbit's rear end. Death doesn't come quickly to take the inflicted. Instead they have to endure a slow, painful decline until either starvation, an opportunist predator or a merciful human being comes along.

But on a more pleasant and optimistic note, enough rabbits are immune to the ravages of the myxomatosis virus, that the species has quite recovered in many areas. There are healthy rabbits about and plenty of them. The rabbit abounds once more and we are fortunate in having these quite remarkable creatures as any of us who have spent any time hunting and observing them in the field will testify. The more the hunter knows about his quarry, the better equipped and able he will be to hunt it effectively, and to give it the respect and admiration it deserves. As with most wild creatures, the rabbit has a highly developed sense of self-preservation and highly developed senses to secure their survival. They need every one of them for they are prey to a whole host of animals and birds of prey. The rabbit is ever on the alert for danger and always ready to warn each other of impending danger.

They have to be eternally on guard for they are vulnerable to predators below as well as above ground. Weasels, stoats, buzzards, goshawks, tawny owls, foxes, badgers and, of course, man and his canine assistants are all queuing up to take the unwary or unlucky rabbit. If a rabbit spots anything strange or threatening, they signal to all rabbits in the area by thumping the ground with one of their very strong hind feet. The underside of their short bob tails are a striking white colour. The sight of this flashing white fur is an unmistakeable danger signal. If, and when, caught the rabbit will also often give a high-pitched squeal. This piercing noise can be heard a long way off and is more than enough to alert all animals out and about that danger threatens. Incidentally, it is also a noise that can startle some young dogs the first time they hear it so be prepared to reassure your inexperienced whippet if he shows signs of concern or alarm.

Nowhere can the rabbit escape his enemies, and his senses have evolved to keep him as safe as possible in what is for the rabbit a very dangerous world indeed. One of the most highly developed of a rabbit's senses is his hearing. His long ears are the most striking aspect of the rabbit's appearance. Measuring up to 7cm long they give the rabbit his distinctive outline and, more importantly, help him to detect the slightest sound and to make sense of his environment. His ears are capable of making tiny and rapid movements to intercept and accurately interpret sound waves as they bounce off objects. The rabbit's ears register his state of arousal. When alert they are bolt upright, flicking to and fro to pinpoint the potential danger. His acute sense of hearing also enables the rabbit to navigate as quickly and easily as possible underground, an environment where his eyes are of little use.

This is also the environment where his sense of touch comes to the fore. This is where his long, delicate and sensitive whiskers come into play. Located around the nose, mouth and on the cheeks above his eyes, they are as wide as his body which lets him gauge the size of entrances and tunnelways without hesitation. With these he can negotiate his way around any underground obstacles and navigate efficiently below ground.

Take a close look at a rabbit's eyes. They are set upon his head in such a way so that he can see almost directly behind his body. This wide field of view serves two purposes; it enables the rabbit to see a predator on the horizon and to decide on the safest escape route. True, it cannot focus as well as the human eye but in its ability to detect movement it is more than fit for its purpose. Their large size allows plenty of light to reach the retina and enables the rabbit to see well even at night. But this is a double-edged sword; for bright intense light quite blinds him, and so a rabbit caught in the headlights of a car or picked up on the lamp has little hope of escape.

His eyesight is good at detecting movement but at the expense of being able to focus in detail and to see things close up. It is thought that he can detect red and green on the light spectrum. Sunset is the safest time for a rabbit to rely on his eyes for this is when they can function at their very best.

With a hundred million scent cells jostling for room in their nose, the rabbit has an exceptionally well-developed sense of smell. He uses the information he gathers with these cells to detect other animals and to identify other rabbits and to help make sense of his immediate environment. Even a newborn rabbit, blind and helpless as he is in so many respects, is nevertheless able to use his nose to maximum advantage and uses it to guide him to his mother's teat and her milk. The nose twitch so characteristic of the rabbit is just him trying to identify an unfamiliar scent.

Taste too helps the rabbit respond appropriately to his immediate environment. He has approximately seventeen thousand taste buds in his mouth and with these he is able to identify a variety of taste sensations: sweet, sour, salty and bitter. Rabbits in captivity have demonstrated this by showing a marked preference for chocolate, sugar and spice and all things nice over their specially formulated rabbit grains. A rabbit in the wild makes a very different use of his sensitive palate and uses it to differentiate between poisonous and edible plants, and to avoid the former.

The body of the rabbit too has evolved to help him evade his predators. He has strong, muscular hind limbs to power him over the ground, with shorter, less powerful front legs to absorb the impact when moving at speed over hard and uneven ground. His mode of movement, the two hind legs in unison and the front ones in quick succession give him great manoeuvrability but at the expense of outright speed. This mode of locomotion can be seen most clearly when you come across the bizarre-looking footprint of a rabbit in the snow. It freezes the movement that cannot be deciphered when watching a rabbit move at speed. At the end of all four feet are some surprisingly sharp and powerful nails which are not only used for digging their holes and homes, but for self-defence and even for attacking other rabbits.

Rabbits are sociable creatures. Bucks, does and their young called kits all live in close proximity to each other. The only difference between the male and female of the species is a small variation in overall size and in the shape of the head. The doe is almost always smaller with a narrower head than the buck. They like to live in colonies, usually but not always, in underground networks known as warrens. The would-be rabbit hunter, then, has to know not only how to find his warrens, but to tell whether they are occupied. Death, disease, too much disturbance, overcrowding can all force rabbits to abandon their homes. If you are not to waste your time and that of your ferret and dog you will need to learn how to tell if anybody is at home. Fresh

Footprints in the snow reveal the rabbit's way of moving.

droppings around the entrance are a sure sign that the holes are being used by rabbits in some shape or form. These are grass green when fresh, other-wise they will be dark.

The rabbit is a herbivore. His teeth easily keep up with his constant grazing activity. His trademark incisors are enamelled almost entirely on the front surface alone and that means they are constantly sharpening them-selves. In fact, the more they are used, the sharper they become. The rabbit produces two kinds of droppings, the hard round 'marble' that we see and a soft night dropping that is rarely seen, chiefly because it is eaten again so that the rabbit can make the most of every blade of grass, can extract and digest every nutrient, vitamin and mineral, and do so in the relative safety of his warren, for grazing above ground for the rabbit is an inherently risky business. By its very nature, the best grass is to be found out in the open where the rabbits themselves become easy prey/sitting targets. This is not quite as repellent as it sounds for the droppings of herbivorous animals are rarely offensive in odour or appearance.

They are mainly nocturnal creatures but can often be seen in the early dawn and twilight hours grazing near their holes Some will even venture out in broad daylight on warm, sunny days or where there is very little disturbance, or when severe weather has kept them underground for a few days.

Despite all the dangers they face on a daily basis, still the rabbit survives. Its ability to breed at a phenomenal rate must have a lot to do with this resilience. It is only their amazing capacity to reproduce that enabled the rabbit to survive the arrival of myxomatosis. The rabbit becomes sexually mature at the tender age of four to five months and are ready, willing and able to mate from this time on. After thirty-one days, the young are born into a nest built by the doe and lined with the soft hair from her own chest and underbelly. Within hours of giving birth the doe is fertile again and is usually mated within days and the cycle begins again until cold weather brings this frenzied sexual activity to a temporary halt. In mild winters, however, breeding can and does go on and can cause quite a few problems for the ferreter. Rabbit kits are easy prey and a ferret stumbling upon a litter can hardly be blamed for helping himself to a free and easy meal while you curse noisily above.

When it comes to breeding time the female rabbit, the doe, digs her own special burrow known as a stop. This she will work hard to prepare for her offspring, lining it with dry grass and the soft fur from her own belly. This specially constructed nursery can either be an extension added to the existing warren or kept completely separate. Rabbits can and do breed at any time given favourably mild weather but the vast majority of reproductive behaviour occurs between the months of January and June. The buck will mate with several does, but will play no role in rearing his young. Each doe will keep within her own territory in the warren concentrating her energy and attention on feeding, cleaning and caring for the rapidly growing young rabbits. It is hard to overestimate the reproductive capacity of the rabbit as a species for it is quite possible for a doe, given favourable conditions, to produce a litter of three to six young every month.

However, maximum productivity is seldom achieved. Even before they are born the young struggle to secure their place in the world. It has been estimated that over half of the young conceived do not survive and are reabsorbed back into their mother's body. Each doe will, on average, produce about ten live young every year. Her young, born underground are blind, deaf and without the protection of any warm coat, and they are reliant on their mother for their survival. She will visit her offspring once a day to suckle and clean them and their nest. When her work is done she will block off the entrance to their tunnel both to conserve heat and to safeguard its inhabitants against enemies. Within a month the young are capable of looking after themselves; after three to four months, they are able to breed and begin the cycle all over again. Given that gestation in the rabbit lasts only about thirty days, the young that are born in one year are ready, willing and able to reproduce themselves several times over by the arrival of autumn.

So what does the future hold for the rabbit? Well, it will undoubtedly continue to face recurrent epidemics of myxomatosis. There will also be new diseases rearing their ugly heads. RHD or VHD, Rabbit or Viral Haemorrhagic Disorder first appeared in Britain in the 1990s in domesticated rabbits but soon spread to their wild cousins. Like its predecessor, myxomatosis, one of the first outbreaks took place in Australia. While it was still undergoing trials for potential use as a biological agent to control a once again burgeoning rabbit population, it escaped from a field trial. Within two months it had killed ten million rabbits.

Unlike myxomatosis the infected animal often shows few external symptoms of the virus. In fact, one recent scientific study suggested that most rabbits with RHD appeared to die a relatively peaceful and painless death. It can be a hard illness to detect, as death occurs quickly, within three days in most cases, and many wild rabbits will die underground. All that the observer will notice is a sudden and marked decline in rabbit numbers in his or her local district.

Where dead rabbits are found, an internal investigation will soon reveal whether RHD is the cause of death. Internally, the rabbit will be a mess. Blood clots will have formed in most or all of the major organs: the heart, lungs, kidneys and liver causing respiratory and/or heart failure. Signs of this are a swollen liver, a black spleen and kidneys stained an unhealthy dark brown colour. Despite its unappetising appearance, and if you can stomach it, meat from these rabbits can be eaten either by humans or ferrets without ill effect.

For an animal that is officially classed as vermin, the rabbit really does taste surprisingly good. At least it does just so long as it is handled right, right from the very start. Like all animals that we hunt to kill, the death should be made as painless and as quick as possible. That means you have to know what you are doing and do it well. Their necks can be broken by a sharp blow to the back of the neck or by breaking it by firmly grasping the legs in one hand, taking hold of the neck in the other, and giving a strong pull. This is not the time for half measures. Set about the task with confidence and put a bit of effort into it and the job will be over in seconds.

Rabbit meat is quickly tainted and soured if the bladder isn't immediately emptied as soon as the rabbit is dead. They can be hung, head down and

You owe it to the rabbit and the whippet's hard work to despatch it humanely.

weather dependent, for four to five days to allow the flavour to develop, but they must be paunched first to keep the flesh clean. Young animals, three to four months old, plump, rounded and tender are the very best for eating and make a delicious meal simply roasted in the oven. Older animals require a little more care, both to dress and to prepare for the table. Done right, however, they too can be just as tasty. Skinning is harder on an older animal especially if he is an experienced old buck. It is these males that are responsible for the reputation the rabbit has for providing strong, unpleasant-tasting meat. When you have one or more of these animals in the larder, you may have to take a little more care in the cooking, but, nevertheless you have some potentially good meat to serve up. Stews and pies are the best place for these rabbits. Slow cooking tenderises the tougher muscle fibres and mellows the flavour.

Apart from providing exceptional sport and good eating, rabbits have several other uses too. Their skins are easy to preserve and make brilliant dummy covers for dog training. Of course, if you have the time, patience and skill you could make yourself a very warm hat indeed.

But despite its classification as a pest species, its very popularity as a hunting quarry might ensure its protection and continued survival. Hunters are the very best guardians of the species that they hunt. Rabbit diseases thrive in overcrowded conditions. The more they are hunted in a responsible way and the more their numbers are sensibly controlled, the healthier the population as a whole will become. The essence and purpose of conservation is, after all, the safeguarding of the species rather than sentimentalising the individual.

8 FIT FOR PURPOSE

It is important to keep your whippet in a fit, healthy condition; fortunately, this is not a difficult thing to do if you set about the task in an informed and organised manner. For a dog to function to the best of his ability he needs to be fit and he needs to be well. When these two requirements are met, you have a remarkable tool and impressive animal to work with.

What can and should we expect from a dog when he is in tip-top condition? His body houses senses, the capabilities of which far exceed our own. Taking the time to learn a little about them will help to guide us as to what is reasonable to expect in terms of their performance. He has a marvellous sense of smell. To appreciate just how marvellous a nose the dog has it helps if we learn a bit about the nose itself. If you are involved in any way with working gundogs, you will often hear it said, usually by their proud owners and handlers that 'such and such a dog has a tremendous nose'. Such a dog may well have a tremendous ability to interpret what his nose is telling him, but they will not be unique in possessing an organ that has a remarkable capacity to make sense of all the scents in the world. It has been estimated that a dog's ability to scent and his sensitivity to smell is perhaps as much as a million times better than our own.

Statistically alone, the dog's nose is a powerful organ. He has about two hundred million olfactory cells compared with the measly five million we humans have. Unsurprisingly he needs and also has a larger area in the brain dedicated to making sense of all this information. This highly developed sense is involved with more than locating quarry; it also helps keep the dog fit and healthy by enabling him to identify and reject unsuitable foodstuffs before they even reach his mouth. His sense of taste is poorly developed as a consequence. A dog has some two thousand taste buds compared to our ten thousand.

The dog's nose and his sense of smell are his windows on the world. His eyesight, therefore, is not quite as keen. In structural terms, the canine eye closely resembles that of the human and both work in the same way. External light enters the eye through the pupil in the centre of the eye and is focused by the lens on to a layer of light-sensitive cells at the back of the eye called

Fit whippets function better in the field.

the retina. From here signals are sent to the brain along the optic nerve. What the dog derives from this information is, however, very different from how humans make sense of these light signals. A dog sees the world in shades of grey and his images are largely black and white. This limited ability to discern and distinguish between colours explains that while you can clearly see the brown rabbit motionless in the grass, your dog can often fail to pick it out. It perceives a grey rabbit against a grey background, for which the rabbit is undoubtedly grateful. The canine eye is relatively poor at perceiving clear images. The lens in a dog's eye is unable to alter shape as much as the lens in the human eye and he may well perceive a far more blurred image of the world. It is also all too easy to forget that the dog's eye level is very different from our own. This is one of the main reasons why I favour whippet dogs over bitches for lamping. There may only be an inch or two in it but that inch can make a big difference when it comes to commanding a better field of view, or rather, view of the field.

But a dog's eye can help him hunt in other, different ways. Their eyes, for example, are particularly good at noticing movement. A stationary rabbit sitting against a grey or brown background may be difficult for the dog to see without possessing full colour vision, but it will be seized upon, and in all likelihood, seized the moment it makes a move. A dog's eyes are also far better suited to see movement at night. A layer of reflective cells called the tapetum in the back of the eye reflects what little light there is available back into the eye, helping to enhance the image. This physiological adaptation is of great help for the carnivore who hunts in the dim light of early morning and evening. Cats, for example, also possess this special layer of cells. Notice next when you see a dog or a cat out at night with a torch or in the headlights of a car; their eyes will appear green or yellow because of the tapetum. Human eyes meanwhile appear red in flash photos as there is a reflection of the blood vessels at the back of the eye.

His sense of hearing too has evolved to help him locate and catch his quarry. He can move his ears independently and is thus able to pinpoint with great accuracy where the sound is coming from. And although his sense of hearing at low levels is similar to ours (we hear little above 20,000Hz), the dog can perceive sounds of well up to 40,000Hz. The use of so-called silent whistles shows just how sensitive a dog's hearing can be. As in humans, this sensitivity declines with age but for the dog in the prime of life, we can always be quiet in our commands, and confident that they can be heard and will be obeyed.

Whippets have the enthusiasm to give a good chase even when they are far from fit. In fact, one of the attractions of the breed is their their willingness and ability to give good show with nothing special in the way of food or exercise. Given the opportunity to exercise every day, they will give themselves a quick workout. But if what you want is a good chase, and a dog with the stamina to give you his best and come home sound, then a bit of preparation is called for.

Even when at play, a whippet gives his all and can do himself damage when executing all his high speed, acute angle twists and turns. They perform all the manoeuvres that they do when in pursuit of their quarry. Rabbits, when they flee do so in zig-zags, not in a straight forward, straight line, and the whippet that is allowed to get seriously out of shape will always be prone to injury.

Both the young dog and the older dog following a long summer lay off will be in need of hardening and allowed time to get prepared for the season ahead. Your whippet will happily spend these warm months soaking up the sun, or avoiding the rain as is far more likely given the vagaries of the British weather. There is certainly nothing wrong with a rest. In fact after a long winter of hard work it can be positively beneficial to have a little time off to rest and recharge both body and mind. But you can have far too much of a good thing. It can be all too easy to forget about your whippet during the quiet summer months, but remember that, while we all benefit from a little holiday, it is unrealistic to expect your dog to put up a good performance in the field after an extended lay off. Plus it is also rather unfair because many injuries are the result of a poorly prepared body being subjected to more strain and stress than they are able to bear. Many injuries in running dogs result from the physical stress of allowing such a dog to engage in fast and high-intensity exercise before they are physiologically ready for the strain it will place on their body. In their heads, whippets are always ready to run and turn, even if they are far from fit in body.

There are several valuable lessons that can be learnt from those most careful and skilful of dog men, greyhound trainers. They have elevated fitness training in their dogs to an art and a science. While the physiology of the greyhound is unique, there are enough similarities between the physique of a whippet and this larger sight-hound, to make these lessons well worth learning and putting into action. The whippet owner has an advantage in that his dog is smaller and therefore far quicker to respond to any fitness regime.

If you allow yourself and your dog about six weeks to get yourselves fit and ready you will not go far wrong. If you count back from when you hope and expect to be getting out after the rabbits in your area, you will know when you need to be starting your fitness programme.

Remember training is more of an art than a science. Guidelines are just that, there to guide you, not lay down the law. It will be largely up to you to formulate and stick to any fitness regime. You will need to read your dog. You will have to develop the ability to take into account how he looks, how

Fit for function.

he moves, how he is feeling and behaving, what his weight is. You will have to take into account and make allowances for the unpredictable and the unreliable. These uncontrollable and frustrating factors include the weather, whether your dog is in season and, last but not least, you, your personal and work commitments. Spending time with your dog and watching him develop physically in front of your very eyes is supposed to be enjoyable and is certainly rewarding.

It is no good being so rigid in your planning that all spontaneity and fun is removed from the process. Physical fitness is not an end in itself. It is no good sticking to a formula if it just isn't working for you or your whippet. It is no good laming your dog, or yourself for that matter. Keep in your mind the ultimate aim of training is to produce an animal in the peak of physical fitness and one that is mentally sharp, not an animal exhausted by relentless exercise before the season even starts. Nor should he be bored of the whole process. Vary your route, get out and about. It is no disaster if you miss a day of work. Whippets have hardy constitutions and forgiving natures, and these are some of the most remarkable things about these working dogs.

The more exercise your dog is doing, the more and better quality food he will need. There is, after all, no point trying to build up your dog's muscle and condition without providing them with all the nutrients, vitamins and minerals the body needs to repair and strengthen itself.

Fast work comes later on in a fitness programme.

Keep your dog's worming programme up to date, obviously. Whereas roundworms were the main enemy of the puppy, from the age of six months, dogs are vulnerable to yet another type of internal parasite, the tapeworm. It grows in segments with the head piece attaching itself to the lining of the intestines. As the sections mature, they detach themselves and they are the rice-like pieces that can be seen in the faeces of affected dogs. Unpleasant and unsightly, they also carry another threat. These mature segments also contain the tapeworm eggs that will continue the cycle once more. And this is not a simple one. Other symptoms are a coat in a poor condition and constant rubbing of the anus, as this is another area where the tapeworm segments accumulate. Roundworms are not usually a problem for the adult dogs but can be encysted in the bitch and activated when she conceives

Given their short coat and regular grooming, whippets are not prone to picking up external parasites, but they can pick them up and if not treated can make life pretty unpleasant for the dog. Unlike the roundworm, the tapeworm requires an intermediate host to perpetuate its life cycle. Fleas are one of the principal couriers of the tapeworm. While it is difficult to make out the flea itself on your dog, its droppings, tiny black specks, are usually far easier to see against the dog's coat and skin. A specially-formulated insecticidal bath should cure the problem. But as fleas are not too fussy about where they lay their eggs, you would be wise to treat his bedding and any furnishings your dog has regularly come into contact with at the same time.

When you worm your dog, make sure you do it properly. Some dogs seem to have an almost uncanny ability to detect a tablet even wrapped up in the most delicious of treats, and spit it out as soon as your back is turned. Mastering the knack of giving a dog tablets is, therefore, vital. Once aquired, your life and that of your dog will be made an awful lot easier and less stressful. Simply put the tablet as far back into the dog's throat as you can. Close his mouth, hold it securely shut and stroke his throat gently until you are sure he has swallowed the tablet.

No animal can perform its best if it is not in the best of conditions, mentally as well as physically. The Roman poet, Juvenal had it about right, when he wrote of the importance of the mind–body relationship. A healthy mind in a healthy body, he declared. And vice versa I would argue. Physical actions can be carried out more rapidly by a sharp, active mind. Mental stimulation requires a little input from the handler but whatever you put in is more than amply repaid in the form of an obedient, contented dog that enjoys all aspects of his life and his work. Bored dogs spell trouble, bored working dogs spell big trouble. All their drive and determination needs to find an outlet somewhere. If their energy cannot be channelled constructively, then these dogs all too often develop destructive habits and adopt difficult behaviour.

It helps if you think of the brain as just another muscle. Admittedly, it is a muscle that cannot be seen and that works in mysterious ways. Nevertheless, it is still one that needs as much care and as much exercise and development as any other. Working rabbits during the winter demands as much mental agility as physical ability. Every situation is different; every encounter with wild animals in their natural environment presents new challenges and obstacles. They all need overcoming, and this requires thought as well as action. Luckily there are many ways you can do this and many long summer months to fill. Use them to make sure your dog comes back stronger, fitter, faster and smarter. You can use them to strengthen his body and develop his mind. With a little imagination you need never run out of ideas.

Memory retrieves are a brilliant way of exercising body and mind. Over the days, weeks and months you can increase the distance, introduce different and more difficult obstacles between the dog and his retrieve. On hot days, you can even involve a bit of water, and although whippets are not great fans of the wet stuff, they will happily wade through small streams and waterways if they can see a point to the exercise.

Getting out and about in all kinds of country.

Roadwalking will form the basis of these early training sessions. This should be slow and steady to build up tough joints, strong tendons, hard muscles and tight feet. Roadwork is good for toughening up the feet and keeping toe nails in good order.

The first two weeks can be spent walking your dog on roads and pavements every day for about an hour plus giving him as much free running as you practically can. Don't venture out in the heat of the day. It is only mad dogs and English men that venture out at such times. Heatstroke, dehydration, and exhaustion are all very real possibilities if you push your dog too hard when it is too hot. Dogs cannot sweat and can only cool themselves by vigorous panting. Although they have a short, fine coat the whippet still shares the dog's inability to sweat and lose heat easily. So if you can't make it out when the day has cooled, it is best to leave any tough physical exertion to another and cooler day.

There are other ways to get out and about with your dog, ways apart from on your own two feet. Pedal bikes are especially useful when you want to pick up the pace without pounding the pavements yourself. Horses, if they are your thing, are another great way to get out and about with your dog. You can be a little more adventurous about the ground you cover when you have four feet underneath you but it does take a little time to make sure horse and dog are at ease in each other's company. Some horses, however quiet they may be in other ways seem unable to resist slipping in a sly kick at an unwary dog. Such behaviour undoubtedly stems from an instinctive distrust for anything that resembles the predatory wolf in appearance, but a rational explanation is of little use when you are faced with a whippet with a broken leg ten miles from home and the nearest help.

Whippets have relatively fine coats and short hair so brushing is certainly not needed to keep their coats in order, but grooming running dogs is not just about vanity and appearance but also about giving your dog's muscles a thorough massaging to give them tone and condition. It is also far more effective in bringing a gleam and deep gloss to any dog's coat, and far better than the quick fix of a shampoo and scrub.

As you hit weeks three and four you can be thinking about building up the distance you are covering over the roads to up to about four miles a day, and gradually set about increasing the speed as much as you are able. And spend longer brushing and massaging.

Weeks five and six should involve making a determined effort to really pick up the pace, cover the ground as fast as you possibly can and follow it by fifteen to twenty minutes of brushing and massaging. Then enjoy a well-earned cup of tea.

The advantage is that such a programme will get you fit and ready for the season too. Field sports are not for the faint-hearted nor do they favour the unfit. There are no 4x4s to ferry the rabbiter about the countryside. His sport will take him up and down dale, often in pretty dire conditions. There may be digging to do and a heavy bag to haul homewards. If you are not fit at the start of the season, then you very soon will be.

The summer can be a quiet few months for the field sports enthusiast. However, for the owner of a working dog there is always an antidote to hand for the boredom felt by both dog and owner. The summer months when breeding rabbits and dense undergrowth make rabbitting an impossible proposition can seem very long and very empty. To remedy this you need to implement a training programme that improves and develops not only his body but his mind, and yours, as well.

The summer is a good time to indulge in a bit of fun and try out something a bit different. This may seem anathema to all working whippet enthusiasts but I'm not talking serious shows here. What I am referring to is those small local village shows where fun and laughter are the name of the game and a rosette and sense of pride the only prizes at stake. Game fairs are great fun and although taken far more seriously by both competitors and crowds alike, at least you can be certain to be among like-minded people and judges with an appreciation of the working dog. And, as the saying goes, a change can be as good as a rest. If nothing else the date of a show can be a good incentive to devise and stick to a fitness regime for nothing catches the eye better than a dog in prime condition, coat gleaming, muscles hardened, bright and brimming with enthusiasm and energy. All the preparation for a show, however small, all helps to foster a sense of pride and purpose in you and your dog.

There is all the fitness work for starters. That is your long-term preparation to get your dog looking and feeling the part. Then you need to help him show off by teaching him how to stand. He should have mastered walking easily on the lead, but if you have neglected this basic part of his education, now is definitely the time to do something about it. No matter how perfect your dog's conformation, no matter how striking he looks in the kennel, if he won't walk properly and stand to be inspected, then no judge will be able to appreciate his qualities. He needs to walk freely and easily with the lead held slack so that it does not interfere with his way of going. When standing he needs to show himself off so all feet square to do justice to a good length of back, head up to demonstrate his length of neck. He needs to be used to being examined by a stranger. The judge will want to examine his teeth to make sure he has the correct scissor bite; he or she will run their hands over his body to check his conformation and physical development. Your dog needs to accept this without any anxiety or stiffness in the body.

Then there are all the night before and morning of the event activities. The washing, the glossing and grooming, the making sure that you have all

Early morning runs are a joy.

you need to enjoy the experience. Schedules, entry fees, leads, bowls, bottles of water should all be packed and ready to go. Don't leave your sense of humour behind either. Judges can make the oddest decisions but however much you may disagree with their judgement, their decision is final and it helps no-one if you make your displeasure all too obvious. The whole experience is supposed to be fun after all. Game fairs are particularly good events for meeting like-minded people. They are a great opportunity to swap notes, exchange anecdotes and catch up on all the local gossip.

The whippet is in general a very healthy and happy breed. They are easy to care for just so long as we know how to set about it in the right way. Running dogs of whatever breed, or combination of breeds, are prone to their own range of health-related problems that come from traversing the ground at high speeds and putting in sharp turns. Whippets are prone to all the stresses, strains, collisions and knocks that come from changing direction at great speed. Do your best to locate a good vet before anything goes wrong, one that understands dogs and running dogs in particular for they really can present some fairly spectacular injuries.

And although obvious and serious injuries are all too easy to diagnose, and can result in lasting and persistent lameness, even relatively minor injuries can alter a dog's balance and physical efficiency. If not noticed right away, these can quickly get worse and lead to far more serious and lasting damage to a dog's muscles and even his bones. If your whippet has taken a serious knock, call him up. Adrenaline will often keep an animal going even when he is injured. The following morning is when stiffness or lameness first appears.

Even fit working dogs can get ill. Dogs, like people, have their off days but sometimes it is a sign that something else far more serious ails them. If in doubt you can take their temperature. Get someone to hold the dog while you carry out what is not a very pleasant procedure. Use a round-ended thermometer for rectal insertion. Apply a little lubricant before you use it and then put it in about two inches and wait two minutes before reading. The normal temperature of a dog is 101.5 degrees fahrenheit (38.5 degrees centigrade). If you note a rise of more than two degrees fahrenheit, get onto your vet.

Dogs benefit from some basic, routine maintenance procedures. Just as regular servicing helps keep a car in good working order, so regular checks on your dog can make all the difference. Make it a rule to run your hands over your dog every day. Do it when he is well and do it regularly and you will learn what feels right, and know when it doesn't. You will soon be able to distinguish between a dog that is in fit condition and a dog that is truly at his peak. There may only be fine differences in muscle tone and condition but you will be able to tell the difference by touch alone. Regular massaging helps you to develop this skill as well as developing your dog's muscle tone and condition. Massaging also helps his skin and coat by helping stimulate the circulation. Rubbing brings out all the natural oils, works dry skin and scurf to the surface where it can be removed with a lightly dampened cloth.

Nails are vital in giving your dog's foot a good grip on the ground. But left to grow too long, they can tear and cause your dog great pain and lasting lameness. Keep his nails regularly clipped. You'll find you'll have to do this more regularly if your dog is in the house or kept on wooden flooring. Concrete runs are fantastic at keeping dog's nails in trim; few of us have an equally hard-wearing floor in our homes. Roadwork is also good for keeping nails in trim. Invest in a good pair of nail trimmers. A strong, sturdy pair should last you for years. More importantly, they will clip neatly and cleanly without leaving a ragged and uneven edge that could cause a running dog problems when moving at speed.

Regular clipping not only prevents some nasty accidents in the field, torn and broken claws for example, it also helps ensure the correct development of the foot. Don't leave it too long between clipping them. Nails contain a vein which moves down as the nail grows so if you have let things get a little out of hand, don't expect to trim the nails back in one go or you risk cutting back into this vein and causing a nasty bleed. Even in normal nails, you should always take care not to clip too far back and needlessly lame your dog. White nails make the job easy as you can see how far down the dark line reaches and stay clear accordingly. Black claws, however, make the job a little trickier and it is better to be too cautious than to cut down too far.

A healthy whippet is a beautiful sight; one that is in peak condition, coat gleaming, eyes bright, standing proud with all his muscles hard and defined is a truly awesome one. It is an image that deserves working for and one that we can be proud of working alongside.

There are no finer companions wherever you are...

9 BREEDING

It's important to ask yourself before you even embark on a breeding programme what you want to achieve. Are you breeding for your own interest, to produce a puppy for yourself, to carry on the line or to improve it. And remember however good you think your dog is there is always room for improvement. Be clear where these areas of weakness are and set out to find a stud dog whose strengths will balance these out. I wouldn't recommend breeding any animal as a money-making scheme. If everything goes well, you might well find yourself in profit at the end but if things don't (and more often that not they don't go quite according to plan) you'll do well to break even. Be prepared for the costs before you start. And be prepared for the time it takes before you begin. Breeding can be a fascinating and very rewarding thing to do but only if it is done with thought, care and time.

Think about where they will be whelped and reared. A litter can be whelped in the house for, during the first two weeks, the puppies will spend their time snuggled up with the dam and she will be quite capable of keeping them clean and under control herself. But even litters reared indoors benefit from a heat lamp. I would even go further and say that they need one. Whippet pups are no more fragile than any other breed, and probably a good deal tougher than most, but direct heat is a must especially while the bitch is still whelping and may be too busy dealing with the business of delivering another puppy rather than making sure her delivered offspring are thoroughly clean and dry. More of all this later but the devil is in the detail. It is as well to be sure before you even take the bitch to the dog that you have the facilities and ability to rear a litter properly.

The really tough time comes when the pups are up and about. Just keeping them clean at this stage is almost a full-time job. A healthy litter of puppies really isn't something most people are ready, willing or able to share their homes with. They will need room to exercise, and it must be easy to keep clean, dry and draught-proof.

And you may well have quite a few puppies to take care of. Despite their relatively small frame, whippets are capable of producing surprisingly large litters. One bitch I owned had ten puppies in her first litter, nine in the next and finished off with eleven for her final flourish. All bar one survived and, I hope, are out there hunting to this day.

Ask yourself what you will do if things go wrong. Whippets usually whelp easily and the vast majority make fantastic mothers but you can't rely on this. In years of breeding I have only had one Caesarean section performed on a whippet bitch, but she lost four of her seven puppies due to the complication and needed a fair bit of help with the surviving three. I shudder to recall how much the whole experience cost in terms of time, money and worry, but these are the things you need to be ready to deal with if you embark upon breeding. Breeding is always something of a lottery but you can lower the odds considerably by getting the right genes in the mix in the first place.

Another good reason not to breed from your bitch until she is physically and mentally mature is to give her the chance to prove her working ability. You won't know what you've got, let alone have an inkling of what you are going to produce. Temperament is not usually a problem with whippets but there are rare occasions when she might be overly shy etc., traits that can be genetic and her fitness for breeding should be seriously considered. Unfortunately, it is rarely the best working bitches that are used for breeding as they are too valuable and too busy working. Yet these are the very bitches we should be breeding from.

She should be fit, well and up to date with her worming and vaccinations, flea control etc. Injuries should not preclude a bitch from being bred from as long as she is strong enough and healthy enough to see it through without risk to her own well-being. How do you assess an injured dog? As one that has an underlying physical weakness that has made them more susceptible to injury or evidence of a particularly hard-going and driven dog. Only a lifetime's acquaintance with the animal in question can provide the answer but it should be asked, and answered honestly if a propensity to injury is not to be perpetuated down the line.

If you have a good dog then it is only natural that you will want to continue the line. The job is, of course, a lot easier if you have a bitch, which helps explain their popularity and their price. Theoretically all you have to do is to wait till she comes in season and then take her along to the nearest whippet dog and hey presto, nine weeks later, out pop a litter of beautiful bouncing puppies. Sometimes for the lucky few this scenario does actually come true. Down the next street there is the best whippet dog that ever lived. He will have put countless numbers of rabbits in the bag, all caught and brought to hand with the softest of mouths. He will, of course, have the perfect conformation, never have been lame or ill and he will be a dab hand at mating a bitch.

Most of us, however, are just not that lucky. The first stumbling block is finding and choosing your stud dog. If you have a good working dog then you owe it to her, to yourself, to whoever else buys your puppies, to find the right one. There might well be a whippet dog around the corner, but chances are he won't be what you want or need in a dog. Maybe he won't have the right pedigree. Maybe he and his ancestors will have been bred for the show bench. Maybe he'll look the business, but will he be up to it when it really counts in the field? If he has never been tried you will never know. And you'll never be sure the pups you breed will be up to the mark either. It takes as much time and money to breed mediocre dogs as it does to breed a litter with exceptional potential. I know which I would like to be known for.

There might be a brilliant working dog but he has no papers. What do you do? I wouldn't use him. It is true that a piece of paper never caught a rabbit, but without it you will never be sure what you are putting into the breed. And just because a dog is a superb worker, unfortunately, this does not mean he will go on to produce his like. If he lacks a depth of working pedigree, if his parents and grandparents were not proven in the field, if he is the product of pure chance rather than good breeding, he will be very unlikely to consistently pass on his qualities to his progeny. Without the paperwork you have no idea what you are putting into your puppies. Neither will anyone who buys them. Bear that in mind when you set your price. Non-registered puppies are worth less than those with proven pedigrees. Breeding dogs isn't the way to make money but it helps if you can at least expect to cover your costs.

Far more likely is you will have to do some homework and legwork to sort yourself out with a good stud dog. It is never too early to start your homework. The breeder of your pup is a good place to start. If they don't have a dog suitable for your own bitch, they might be able to recommend one that is. If you see a dog you like don't be afraid to ask about studs. Get a copy of the pedigree if you can. Get a feel of what lines are out there and how they perform. How do they knit into your own bitch's pedigree? What are you trying to produce? Do you want to pep up her hunting? Develop a stronger retrieving instinct? Perhaps you are looking to bring the size up a little, or bring it down? No dog is perfect but it is the breeder's duty to get as close to the ideal as possible.

Try not to be offended if the owner of the dog asks to see a copy of your bitch's pedigree and/or the bitch herself. Most are very polite about it and are merely trying to safeguard their reputation and maintain the quality of the breed. Instead you should be reassured that here is someone that treats breeding with the seriousness it deserves. Every time you breed a dog of whatever breed, you have a chance to give something back to the breed. You can either contribute or detract from it, as you are in control of the genetic ingredients that go into your litter. You can't determine the exact mix but you can do all you can to make sure that you are producing quality specimens of the breed. You should be looking to improve on the dog you have, or at the very least to maintain excellence. This is by no means an easy thing to do which is what makes breeding such a fascinating and challenging business. Remember that in any mating, the genes your puppy will inherit will come in equal measure from both parents. The best dog in the world won't correct the failings of the worst bitch and vice versa.

The best recommendation is what the dog has already produced. If you like that then chances are you'll like your litter. Plus chances are, you will actually get a litter. Not all dogs, nor all bitches are fertile and some are a lot more potent than others. Proof is in the pudding, or rather in producing puppies. An experienced dog is always best especially if you have a maiden or a nervous bitch. He will know the job and so will his owner. If you are going to an inexperienced dog and you really do want to produce a litter, you can arrange a back up. It can be hard to find a dog at short notice if you haven't given the matter some thought beforehand. But be tactful and discreet about it, as no owner wants to think his dog is being treated as second best.

Now to the nitty-gritty of the matter. Money. There are several variations on the theme but expect to pay for the service of a stud dog. These range from money for the mating itself, irrespective of whether the bitch has puppies or not. Some stud dog owners are happy to offer a free mating if the bitch is found not to be in pup this time round, and some want a puppy and will stipulate the pick of the litter. Both arrangements have their advantages and disadvantages. Whatever arrangement you decide upon, make sure both parties are completely clear about what it entails. It is always best to have it all down in writing so there is no room for future disagreement and dissatisfaction.

For registration purposes, the bitch should have been at least a year old when she was mated. For her own health and well-being she should be at least two years old. Giving her this extra time to mature and develop gives her a chance to fulfil her potential on the field and prove that she really is worth the time and effort involved in breeding a litter.

At the other end of the spectrum, the Kennel Club will not register puppies from a bitch that has already had six litters nor if she is already eight years old when she has the puppies. So if you want to breed pedigree whippets and register their progeny, you have a limited time frame in which to do it.

Let's assume your bitch is healthy, well, and well within the time frame allowed. You notice that she has come into season. What do you do? Well, make a note of the date. If you are anything like me, in the hurly burly of life, you will forget when it was and have to spend hours trying to figure out that she must have come into season because it was in between taking little Johnny to stay at Fred's house and picking William up from his swimming lesson that you noticed that your bitch was looking a bit swollen. Or was it when you had that dentist appointment? It is always at times like this that I heartily regret not picking up a pen and jotting it down on the calendar.

Most bitches come into season every six months but some only do so once every twelve months. Most are fairly regular, but not all. All you can do is keep a careful record of when and for how long her seasons' last to try and figure out her cycle. A bitch's oestrus cycle can be understood better if we take the time for a bit of science and if we break the whole thing down into different stages.

The process begins when you first notice her vulva is swollen and that there is a blood-stained discharge. She will be receptive to any male dogs she encounters and may even try to seek male company out. However, she will not be willing to take the matter further than flirtation. The next stage, oestrus, is when the discharge from her vulva changes colour from red and blood-stained to a clear or very light yellow shade. This is when she ovulates or releases her eggs and this is when she is at her most fertile. The window of maximum fertility lasts between thirty-six hours and five days, although it varies from bitch to bitch and from one year to the next.

A bitch is usually in season for around twenty-one days. This is counted from when she begins to show a blood-stained discharge from her vulva. This too will be swollen. A lot of bitches will urinate more often during and just before they come into full season and this can give you a bit of advance notice. She will only be fertile for a relatively short time during this period so you need to keep a careful watch and note of dates and times. As a general guide most bitches are ready to be taken to the dog when the discharge turns from pinkish-red to almost clear. This is a sign that she has released her eggs and will accept being mated by a dog.

Most bitches are fertile around day eleven but this is only a very rough guide and it can vary enormously. Some are ready for the dog much earlier or much later. There are certain physical signs and some behavioural ones that give a good guide to when she will be ready to take to the stud dog. The bleeding from her vulva will have stopped to be replaced by a clear discharge. She will no longer seem quite so red around this region. Bitches will usually give a pretty clear indication themselves that they are ready and willing to be mated by their reaction to the presence of another dog. She will stand stock still and turn her tail to make mating as easy and inviting as possible. It is also as well to remember that dogs and bitches can be quite proactive in the whole business of procreation and will be drawn like magnets to each other when the time is right. And a bitch is not fussy when it comes to finding a partner at such times. Next door's mangy mongrel will do, so be aware of this and keep an eagle eye on her at all times. And remember your vigilance shouldn't end once she has been mated by a dog of your choosing. During her window of fertility she can mate with more than one dog and have puppies by both fathers too. Rare but not, unfortunately, impossible.

It is a help and gives peace of mind, if the owner of the stud dog will give a second mating, as part of the original stud arrangement of course. Also remember that sperm stays fertile in the body of the bitch for up to five days after the mating although its potency declines significantly after the first twenty-four hours.

If you are travelling any distance or just want peace of mind, then there is a blood test available from your veterinary surgeon that will tell you exactly when your bitch is ovulating and releasing her eggs. Yes, it costs money but it is up to you to put a price on your peace of mind.

Everything is in place and you head off to your stud dog. What should you expect? Well, the owner of the stud dog should take charge of the dog leaving it up to you to ensure your bitch behaves. Unsurprisingly most stud dog owners take a fairly dim view of bitches, or owners who allow their bitches, to show aggression. An experienced dog might well shrug off such treatment, a younger or more sensitive soul might be put off his stride for your bitch, if not all bitches. Take a muzzle if you are in any doubt and don't be offended if the owner of the dog asks you to use one. It's far better for all concerned to be safe rather than sorry. Maiden bitches are particularly prone to nerves but even older bitches when they are ready for the dog can show a decidedly nasty side. It is, after all, quite a stressful experience for her. Be firm but reassuring. A muzzle will take care of the teeth, you might have to keep the rest of her under control.

Things get a lot tougher when you have a reluctant or inexperienced dog and a similar bitch, which is why I strongly recommend that at least one of the dogs involved knows the job well. An experienced dog will waste no time with a bitch if she isn't ready or has stopped ovulating. While this can be frustrating at the time, it does save a lot of wasted effort and disappointment. A little bit of free time in the garden away from distractions gives both dogs a chance to assess each other and relax. Don't interfere unless the bitch shows obvious signs of aggression and/or fear. Neither are very likely but it is as well to keep an eye on the proceedings. Then proceed only once you are happy that the dogs are responding well to each other.

Most bitches, when the time is right will take the whole thing calmly and willingly, turning their tail and standing still. And the stud dog should do the job with enthusiasm. Once the energetic part is over and done with and the dogs have tied, he will usually try to dismount and turn so that his rear end and that of the bitch face each other. This is a delicate operation and the stud dog owner should be on hand to assist to prevent injury and minimise any discomfort for both parties concerned.

While the act of mating seems simple enough it is actually quite a complex business. It can be divided and described in three stages. During stage one, semen is passed into the bitch, a process that takes just a few seconds. Stage two lasts for a few minutes and passes the sperm. The third and final phase is the gradual discharge of seminal fluid helping send the sperm along their merry way. During all these stages, the bitch and the dog will be tied together. This rather uncomfortable looking arrangement is brought about by both partners. At the very base of the dog's penis is a gland, the bulbus glandi, a gland which swells during the act of mating and is then held by the

A good tie, well under control.

Not long until whelping.

vaginal muscles of the bitch. Until this swelling subsides the bitch and the dog cannot physically be parted and injury will result if the issue is forced upon them. A tie can last a long time and the dogs will need constant supervision so it helps if you have somewhere comfortable to sit, preferably somewhere under cover if the weather is bad. Very short ties or slip-matings, that last only a few minutes, or less, can also be successful but they do leave you feeling a little unsure about the whole affair.

Gestation in the dog lasts on average nine weeks or sixty-three days. For most of that time it will be hard to tell whether the bitch is in whelp or not. For the first few weeks after mating at least the bitch will need no special care. There is no need to feed her more, or unduly restrict her exercise other than trying to avoid any knocks and collisions that might cause her to abort any fertilised eggs. And remember a fat dog is not a healthy dog and certainly not a fertile one.

Most bitches begin to show definite signs of being in pup at about six weeks. Teats will start to be more prominent, they will lose their waist. For a while it may just look like they have a full belly before it becomes unmistakably a belly full of puppies. She will slow down but it is up to you to make sure she has no serious mishaps and comes to no harm during this period. Also if she is in the house you will find that she needs to go out more often to relieve herself and you may find that for the first time since she was house-trained, you start to have the odd accident again. In fact, you (and she) might find it easier, if it is possible, to move her out into a kennel for the week before she is due to whelp. Some bitches find being out quite upsetting but if you have other dogs in the house she will probably appreciate the peace and security. Her days can still be spent in the house if you are there to keep an eye on her, but it is safer for the bitch and the puppies if she is in her whelping box with the heat lamp at night. Even in the summer, she should have this facility. Make sure the heat lamp is just low enough to warm the floor of the box without interfering with the bitch's freedom of movement. Expectant mothers can become very restless before and during whelping and the last thing she will need at this crucial time is a metal lamp getting in her way.

Maiden bitches often whelp early, up to five days sometimes, so be prepared for this eventuality. Dig out or get hold of a good infra red heat lamp and have at least one spare bulb to hand. You don't want to be rushing to the shops late on a Friday night in search of one while your pups shiver. Cold won't necessarily kill them but it will put them under undue stress. It may well retard their growth, and certainly give them a knock. All their energy will be put into staying warm rather than growing and developing. Get in a supply of suitable bedding. Stock up on old newspapers, you will be surprised how many you will get through.

For the same reason her whelping box should be draught free. The pups will be unable to move and the bitch will be unwilling to leave her precious charges. Her energy will go into keeping herself and her puppies warm at the expense of producing plenty of milk.

Her whelping box doesn't need to be expensive or complicated, just big enough for her to stretch out in but not so big that the puppies risk wriggling too far away. It is vital that it is draught-proof but well-ventilated. There should be no nails sticking out that could cause injury to the puppies or the bitch. The sides need to be high enough to stop any draught but not too high that the bitch could injure herself and damage her teats getting in and out. A 'U' shape cut out of one side can assist the bitch in getting in and out but should not allow the puppies to crawl or fall out. It should be easy to clean out and to keep clean. A piece of old carpet cut to fit the exact size and then securely attached to the base of the box with large-headed nails makes a good insulating layer. Fixing it to the floor stops puppies managing to wriggle underneath and suffocate.

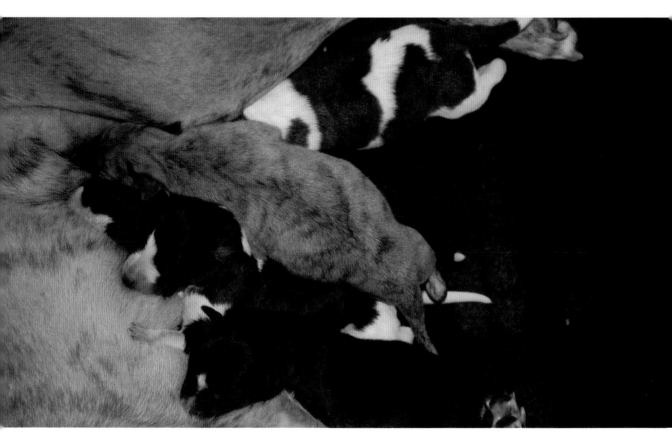

A content litter of puppies with full bellies.

You will need to have somewhere in mind and somewhere prepared for your bitch to whelp and rear her puppies. Whether indoors or outside, one thing your bitch will appreciate is peace and privacy. If you can observe things without being noticed yourself, if you can peep in on the proceedings, so much the better. That is not to say that you should just put her in a pen and let nature take its course. Things can and do go wrong and you should be on hand at all times to assist if needed. In the house give her a spot away from the hustle and bustle of everyday family life and in particular from the prying eyes and fiddling fingers of small children.

Wherever she is to go, don't leave introducing her to these new surroundings until the last minute. At least a week before she is due to whelp move her into her temporary new home. She will probably appreciate the peace and the privacy and be better able to concentrate on the task in hand.

The signs of impending whelping are many and varied. The bitch will usually go off her food the night before. She may well seem restless and uneasy. She will in all likelihood try and scratch up her bed and to make a nest for her newborn litter. She may get up, sit down, move about and refuse to settle. It's hard to say what is normal in whelping other than the puppies all come out safe and well in a reasonable time scale. Your gut instinct is a good guide but if you have any doubts or are worried about how things are going, don't hesitate to get expert help.

Whippets normally whelp without difficulty but the odd problem does arise. I am a firm believer in leaving well alone unless the bitch is in distress and discomfort. Whelping is a mentally taxing and physically tiring business; the last thing a healthy bitch during a normal birth wants is needless interference. I see little point in weighing each and every puppy the moment it is born. It is soon obvious if any are noticeably smaller or not putting on enough weight or keeping pace with their litter-mates. The bitch should clean and dry the puppies herself, and in the normal course of events there is no need to dive in with a towel as soon as each new puppy is born. I think it is far better to allow the bitch to bond with each new arrival, removing the birth sac and cutting the umbilical cord. Besides, the suckling and gentle pawing of the newborn puppies stimulates the production of the hormone, oxytocin. This acts to strengthen the bitch's contractions and encourages the let down of milk into her teats. A baby monitor left after the rearing of my own children has been given a new lease of life and is great for giving peace of mind.

The early stages of labour are all about the muscles of the cervix dilating until they are large enough to allow the passage of a puppy. This can take anything from half an hour to three or four. However, always take professional advice. Far better to contact your vet than risk something going seriously wrong. When a bitch is whelping what you will see first is the water

She will also deal with the umbilical cord.

bag, which contrary to expectations looks almost black and filled with fluid. The puppy itself might appear head first or legs first. Breech births are rump-first presentations and do not necessarily cause problems but if the bitch is tired this slightly awkward presentation can cause problems.

More and more people seem to be having their bitches scanned to determine if and how many puppies she is carrying. This can help put the owner's mind at risk and help determine whether your bitch is experiencing that most baffling and frustrating phenomenon, the phantom pregnancy. Her hormones are telling her brain and her body she is pregnant when she isn't. It has been suggested that it harks bark to the wolf pack where submissive bitches who would not be mated themselves would have milk to suckle the alpha female's pups should anything happen to her or prevent her from providing for her own litter. Some bitches really do look and behave as if they are in pup, even produce milk, make nests, lick toys clean. It is all very upsetting but all usually returns to normal two or three weeks after the 'due' date. One comfort is that just because she, and you, have gone through one phantom pregnancy, this won't impinge on her ability to conceive at the next mating.

Unfortunately no chapter concerned with breeding dogs would be complete without mentioning some of the things that can and sometimes do go wrong. Thankfully, mishaps and mal-presentations are few and far between as far as the whippet is concerned. But it is as well to have a working knowledge of what to look out for and what to do if you do encounter any serious problems. It goes without saying to have your vet's number to hand. As with all professions, there are good vets and bad vets. Make sure you know which is which in your area; if your bitch is good enough to breed a litter from then she deserves the best of treatment.

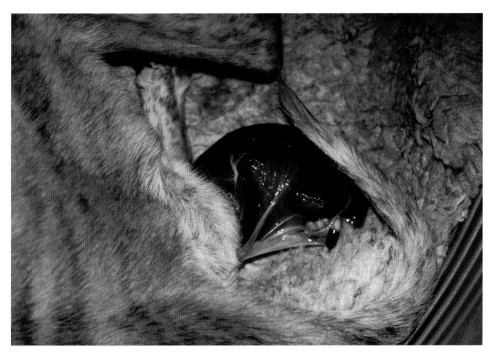

A rear presentation rarely presents any problems.

10 THE NEXT GENERATION

The first three weeks of rearing a litter are among the easiest, for you at least. For the bitch they will be the most demanding, physically and mentally. It is perfectly feasible and even enjoyable to have a litter in the house up until this age. They will spend their time eating, sleeping and growing. Once they become mobile, the situation changes dramatically. It can be a revelation even to the most experienced breeder to let a bitch whelp in the house. You will see and hear the litter develop before your very eyes.

Up until this point you should concentrate on the bitch, on keeping her well fed with top quality food and plenty of clean, fresh water to drink. Producing milk is a physically exhausting business. And taking care of puppies can be mentally taxing too. You might well notice a marked change of character, and your once bold and outgoing bitch becomes a mouse of a thing. You are no longer the centre of her world at least in these early days. Keep a careful eye on any children that they are not too rough, too noisy, or get too close. She should have a quiet spot, away from the noise and chaos of normal human family life. She will decide when she is ready to rejoin her family pack, and it doesn't usually take long.

For the first day or so after whelping she will probably need to empty her bladder and her bowels more often than usual so there will need to be some-one around fairly often to let her out, or she will need access to somewhere to relieve herself. If an accident happens, don't be hard on her. She has enough on her plate with a litter of hungry demanding puppies.

Monitor the behaviour of the puppies. They should be evenly spaced. If they are huddled together, they are too cold and the heat lamp should be lowered and the box checked for any unwelcome draughts blowing through. If they are pressed to the far sides of their box, then they are too hot and the lamp should be raised up. Remember the bitch can escape from either of these extremes; her puppies are far less fortunate. Noises are normal but continuous noisy squealing is usually a sign of distress.

Any noticeably weak and/or small puppies should be given particularly close attention. For the first twenty-four hours I am willing to give these puppies a bit of extra help; putting them on the bitch's teat at frequent intervals etc but if they still show no noticeable sign of improvement or fight for life, then I'm afraid I make no apology for putting them down. A whippet not only loves to run, it lives to do so. To keep any alive that are not firing on all cylinders seems a cruelty to the individual dog and a disservice to the breed itself. It is far better for the bitch and you to give your undivided attention to the healthy members of the litter. Now I'm not talking about the runt of the litter which may be small but comes out fighting. These particular puppies often show a courage that far exceeds their size and your expectations, and many continue to do so for the rest of their lives. No, these rarely need help and if they have a shaky start, being popped onto a teat once or twice soon sets them on their way.

For the first few days after birth, your puppies will be deaf and blind, and they will spend the first two weeks eating and sleeping. They will interact with their environment through the sense of touch, smell and sensitivity to hot and cold. The bitch will keep them clean by regularly licking their tummies; this encourages evacuation and the bitch will, in turn, lick up the urine and faeces. It is a natural act to keep the den or nest clean. In the third week the senses start to develop. They are able to use their tiny noses to greater effect and interpret what it tells them more easily. Their eyes will begin to open from about day twelve, first as tiny slits, then bright black beads. The world will not suddenly be revealed to the puppy in glorious technicolour; instead the acquisition of sight will be a more gradual process. They will also start to react to strange noises as their sense of hearing develops and look to find the source of the sound. Equipped with more able brains and bodies, the young animal's natural sense of curiosity and exploration will emerge and he will begin to move around the bed.

The puppies' dew claws should be removed on the third day. It is absolutely vital that this minor operation is done, and done well. A vet can do it if you are not confident and capable of doing it yourself. Getting it wrong or not doing it soon enough will inevitably mean a trip to the vet anyway and a costly operation under anaesthetic both financially and in terms of the dog being out of action for quite some time. All three joints of the dew claw need to be removed cleanly and quickly. Sharp, curved scissors are the best tool for the job and should be sterilised beforehand by boiling in water.

The best advice I have ever had about rearing puppies was to keep a pair of sharp nail scissors on hand at all times and to keep the puppies' nails clipped. Their nails can become like razors which they slash at the poor bitch's teats. No wonder so many turn decidedly nasty to their pups after a prolonged period of this treatment.

A good first litter for a bitch; not too many and nicely marked.

During the excitement of the new arrivals and the developing puppies, make sure you don't neglect to give their dam the care and attention she needs and deserves. Aside from the general wear and tear of producing enough milk to feed a litter of hungry growing puppies, she will be at risk. Don't take your eye off the ball or rather, off the bitch. Two conditions in particular need to be looked out for.

Eclampsia or milk fever is a nasty and potentially life-threatening condition. If this is caught in time, it should be easy to cure. Speed really is of the essence here to deal with this condition that is caused by a sudden and dramatic drop in the calcium levels of the bitch's blood. She will become at first tottery and unsteady on her feet, and her behaviour will become increasingly erratic and unusual. Fits soon follow and unless rapid action is taken and the right treatment given, the bitch will almost certainly die.

Calcium is one of the most important minerals required for growth by any animal. It is required particularly for the correct development of bones and teeth. Before the puppies are born it is supplied through the dam's blood stream and after they are born directly through her milk. Consequently the bitch's calcium reserves are constantly being drained by her developing embryos and her growing puppies. This demand is especially acute from around the fifth week of pregnancy up until she has finished feeding the puppies. Milk fever results from a sudden and dramatic shortage of calcium in the pregnant or lactating bitch. And while it can occur during the pregnancy it is far more likely to affect her during the second or third week after her puppies are born and when the puppies are making the greatest demands on her milk, and consequently, calcium reserves.

The symptoms of this very serious condition include a nervous restlessness, unexplained stumbling, a stiffening of the legs, and finally the bitch lies down on her side, kicking often with her whole body going into violent spasms. These fits can wear off but will undoubtedly recur if the correct treatment is not sought and given very quickly. Without help from a vet who will inject calcium directly into her blood stream to replace her depleted stores, the bitch is highly likely to die of heart failure or exhaustion. In almost all cases the bitch recovers very quickly. Your vet will be best placed to advise what after care should be given to the affected bitch but, if it is at all possible, do not let her feed the puppies for a day or so to allow her body to recover its strength fully. With careful and proper feeding during the latter stages of pregnancy and when lactating, milk fever is unlikely to occur, but if it does, get veterinary help and get it straight away.

You should also be on the constant look out for mastitis. Is an inflammation of one or more of the mammary glands and can affect all lactating mammals. It is not hard to detect. Her teats will become hot and hard to the touch and the bitch will often object to being touched in this highly sensitive and painful area either by you or her puppies. The milk being produced in the inflamed mammary glands will be discoloured and might even be stained with traces of blood. The bitch herself may also show signs of fever, lethargy and general unhappiness. Gently pressing warm, damp towels and expressing the milk at regular intervals might give her some relief, but this will only be palliative and antibiotic treatment will almost certainly be required.

If you are going to register the puppies, get onto it as soon as possible. Once you are certain that all the puppies in the litter look fair to survive, then you can get on with the unpleasant task of filling in all the paperwork. This is especially important if you are planning to sell some or all of the puppies. Come eight weeks when the puppies are ready for their new homes, you will be cursing the late arrival of the documents. Pedigrees should be written out neatly and individually for each puppy. Your address and phone

It is a big world for a small puppy.

number gives the new owners a chance to stay in touch and let you know how things are going. Good or bad, any breeder will appreciate feedback.

By three weeks old your puppies will have developed enormously, from the helpless creature that the bitch whelped, and they will now be able to see, hear and smell fairly well. They will also be more mobile and developing their strength by exploring their surroundings. Now is the time to get them outside in a run. They will need more room to exercise and to indulge in plenty of play. Plus remember that when weaning commences, the dam will stop cleaning up after the puppies, so you have to take over the hard task of keeping the bed and run clean at all times.

At around three weeks of age the first teeth begin to break through and solids can be introduced. Now is around the time to begin weaning, and learning to eat can be a very messy business. The bitch's milk, while still highly nutritious, is no longer quite enough to satisfy the appetite and demands of a rapidly developing puppy. Nor can a bitch be expected to keep up with such demands. Lactation and nursing puppies take their toll on the dam and around this time she will also be grateful for a bit of assistance in meeting the demand of her puppies. Should you have any reluctant feeders, keep a close eye on them but try not to pander to them and pamper them, but instead harness their competitive instincts and feed the puppies from a communal bowl. It will be easy to see if any are not getting their fair share.

You should make the transition to solids a gradual affair. Start off with soft, easy to eat and easy to digest foods. Scrambled egg is always popular and usually wolfed down without any hesitation. Healthy puppies will rarely need any encouragement to clear their bowl. After a few days on this simple diet you can introduce specially formulated puppy food. Soak it well in plenty of water overnight until it resembles a soft, crumbly pulp. Your puppies will be very messy after tucking into this nutritious mix but they will be well and truly satisfied, for the time being at least. Over the years I have sought out the ultimate dish with which to feed puppies. I have tried large heavy earthenware dishes but little legs and tails can be trapped under them in the melee of a large litter. Finally I have settled upon large rectangular trays, similar to those used in catering and for transporting school dinners. They are easy to keep clean and allow all the puppies easy access to their meals.

Feed plenty, feed good food, and feed as often as possible and give your puppies a chance to grow into dogs you can be proud of.

Now the best food in the world and large amounts of it are not going to do your puppies much good if you neglect to keep on top of worm infestation. Roundworms or ascarids pose a particular danger to puppies. If present in any number they can be seen in their droppings. The signs of a heavy worm infestation are impossible to miss: a dull coat, a bloated distended stomach beneath and a prominent spine above. And just because none of the above symptoms are present, it doesn't mean that the worms themselves are not, and are not doing damage. Part of the life cycle of the roundworm is spent in the bitch herself and these particular parasites can be passed to the embryo puppies through the placenta. Puppies are infested with roundworms before they are even born.

Even if the bitch has been regularly wormed for roundworms and tapeworms, assume that at least some roundworms have quite literally wormed their way into the unborn puppies, and treat the litter accordingly, and strictly according to instructions. Failure to worm regularly all too easily leads to a vicious circle; even a small infestation in the puppies will be ingested by the bitch when she cleans them and so the cycle begins again. Plus you run the risk of eggs etc being picked up and passed onto humans. Children are especially vulnerable, another very important argument for staying on top of worming. It should begin when the puppies are two weeks old and since not all the worm larvae grow at the same rate a second dose of medicine must be given at two-week intervals thereafter.

Hard work begins when the bitch's testing time is nearly done. Once the puppies are eating food readily, I see no reason to delay weaning. I also see no reason to delay getting dam and litter outside into more spacious accommodation. Keeping puppies clean and well outdoors is still hard work but at least you can employ a shovel and brush and hosepipe to stay on top of the work. Puppies often do better once weaning has begun and the bitch can be taken away for increasing periods of time. Unless the litter is small, and whippets commonly have large litters, they will usually be beginning to run a little short of milk. With the best will in the world and all the best food, the bitch will be struggling to produce enough milk to satisfy the voracious and insatiable appetite of her offspring. As they get older, they get rougher, tougher and a lot readier to use their newly found teeth on their poor dam's battered teats. Cuts and scratches are the most common cause of infection and mastitis in a bitch so you will be doing her a favour at least if you give her some time out. Slowly increase it until she is out all day and back in again only at night. When she is not there, the pups can have ad lib good quality food and then they really will pile on the pounds.

Socialisation is another aspect of rearing puppies that should never be neglected. This takes a lot of work and effort. Introducing your puppies to the wider world around them and to the human world that they will be part of for the rest of their lives simply cannot be skimped upon. If this crucial learning period is lost, the time can never be made up. From four to seven weeks a puppy is busy learning how to be and behave like a little dog. At this age wolf pups will start to clamber out of their nest and to venture out of the den for short periods of time. The more adventurous puppies of domesticated dogs will show the same instinct to explore and may well scramble out of their box. Learning is intense during this period and all experiences rapidly and easily assimilated. It is, therefore, vital that the puppies must see and hear as much as they possibly can of other dogs and of humans too. Scientific experiments have shown that if a puppy is isolated from canine and human contact for these vitally important three weeks, then they cannot help but remain anti-social with members of their own species and shy around humans. Get as many people as you can involved in spending time with the puppies; play with them, handle them and talk to them. The more you put in now, the more there will be for their future owners to draw

Puppies just love to explore.

out. You are investing in their future and in your reputation as a breeder of quality dogs.

Learning does not stop after this. Between eight and thirteen weeks the young puppy begins to learn its place in the canine community and how to behave accordingly and appropriately. Some will accept their status without demur, while others will fight for theirs. The dam will begin to play far more roughly now for what she is doing is preparing her offspring to respect adult dogs, how to be corrected and how to play their role in the family pack. This play period with the bitch is extremely important for the puppies' development.

I know this from experience. When my first son was a year old he trapped his finger in a door and spent some time in hospital while the damage was put right. While all this was going on I had a litter of young pups growing up at home. Helpful friends and family made sure they were well fed and watered. They were a picture of health and well-being when I got back to them. While in their run, in the comfort and security of their own surroundings and with their litter-mates they were bold and boisterous, but outside, they were shy, timid and took a long time to learn basic human and canine social skills.

If you are planning to keep a puppy back from the litter then you will have been watching them like a hawk from the moment they were born. Often there is one that stands out but that can and does change over time. The pup that was the pick of the litter at two, three, even four weeks might not stand out at all when crunch time comes. This close and continuous observation is one of the joys and the advantages of breeding your own dog.

Bidding farewell to a litter you have bred and reared can be quite a poignant experience. There is always a tinge of sadness to see puppies that you have watched being born and grow depart. But there is pleasure too at a job well done and a sense of shared anticipation and excitement about what these young whippets will achieve when they begin serious work with their new owners. There is also a sense of relief. Rearing puppies is an absorbing activity but it is a serious responsibility and it can be seriously exhausting. In the kennel there is a seemingly endless round of feeding, worming, cleaning and socialising to get done. But the job doesn't end there. If you are registering your puppies with the Kennel Club then there is paperwork to be seen to, records to be kept for your own personal interest and information. Adverts will be written, queries and questions responded to and answered. Finding the right homes for your carefully bred and reared working whippet puppies is a time-consuming task in itself.

Breeding and rearing a litter of puppies for the first time can be a steep learning curve and is a time-consuming project, but it is not a complicated one. Certain simple rules should be adhered to. Keep your bitch fit and well,

Puppies love play.

and well fed, and supply her puppies with warmth and plenty of high quality food. Keep them free of parasites on the inside and the outside. Give them plenty of space to find their feet and to develop their confidence. And invest as much of your time as possible into producing happy, balanced animals, full of enthusiasm for life and ready to do you credit in their new homes and careers. It is richly rewarding and deeply satisfying to produce working whippets worthy of the name, and it is an achievement of which to be proud.

Conclusion

There is a joy and a zest for life that is peculiar to the working dog alone. And there is a deep pleasure and lasting satisfaction in working with dogs. Put the two together and you have taken some large steps towards a richly rewarding life.

Whippets are working dogs. If you understand and make good use of this very important part of his make up and his character, then you will learn so much more about your dog than you ever thought possible. He will show resourcefulness and resilience in greater measures than you ever dreamed.

You will both play a part in the glorious natural world and all that goes on there, and you will take your place among the hunters and the hunted of the wild animal kingdom. You will see, hear and experience sights and sounds that few humans ever encounter and you will gain insight beyond your imagination. You will be part of a world so much larger, richer and endlessly fascinating than our own small human one. Troubles fade and worries recede. Whatever the bag, whatever the weather, time spent out and about in the natural world is never time wasted. And if all that doesn't inspire you to get out there and get working with your whippet, then nothing will.

A good dog is something to be proud of, and justly so. It is not the result of chance alone, but of months of careful training and preparation and years of work. That is not to say that training a dog is all work, work, work. Far from it. All work and no play don't just make Jack no fun to be around, but also takes the joy out of a whippet and his owner.

There is so much that you can't teach a dog, and that you can't teach a dog owner either. Some lessons can only be learnt, or learnt well, through experience. The aim of this book has been to help the owner prepare himself and his dog and to give them the confidence to get out there and get this experience. The best dogs never stop getting better. The best dog handlers and hunters never stop learning. That is what makes sharing a working life with a dog immensely satisfying, richly rewarding and endlessly exciting.

There is a downside to owning the dog of your dreams. Their lifespan is a lot shorter than we human's three score and ten, and their working time is over all too soon. There comes a time when all dog owners will have to make a hard decision on behalf of his companion, to bring to end a life that is no longer worth living. Whippets love life, but they love a life they can live, not one they are forced only to watch from the sidelines. No dog should have to suffer the pain and indignity of a prolonged and painful decline. No owner of a dog should put their dog through this either. When the time comes, a responsible owner will do the right thing and will ensure that it is done well with as little distress and discomfort as is possible.

But your dog can live on in his offspring. If a dog is worth working and has proved his worth, then it is worth making the effort and investing the money in breeding your own replacement puppy. This is certainly not an option for the faint hearted; breeding dogs is certainly not the way to turn a quick buck but if undertaken with open eyes, careful thought and a passion to produce the very best examples of the breed, mentally as well as physically, it is a fascinating experience. A healthy litter of puppies, well reared, socialised and settled in good homes, is an achievement to be proud of.

If the whippet had not had men and women over the years willing to sacrifice their time and their money to improve and consolidate the very best qualities of the breed, then none of us today could enjoy the beauty, power and infectious love of life and hunting that the working whippet brings to all who are fortunate to share his life.

INDEX